Copyright © 2025 by James Kaddis

All rights reserved. No portion of this book may be reproduced, stored in a retrieval system, or transmitted in any form or by any means—electronic, mechanical, photocopying, recording, or otherwise—without prior written permission of the publisher, except for brief quotations in reviews or articles. Published by JNK Productions LLC.

All Scripture quotations are taken from the King James Version of the Bible.

ISBN (Hardcover): 979-8-218-87211-3
ISBN (KDP Softcover): 979-8-242-87117-5
eBook ASIN B0G54JP4VJ

Cover design, interior design and typesetting: Authorentic℠.

Printed in the United States of America.

JNK Productions LLC

A GUIDE TO REVELATION: PART ONE

WHAT YOU NEED to KNOW
ABOUT REVELATION,
the RAPTURE, and the END TIMES

JAMES KADDIS

This book is dedicated to the One who inspired me to write it, the God of Heaven, the one and only true God, the God of Abraham, Isaac, and Jacob. He saved me, gave me the hope of eternity, and established true purpose in my life. He has given me every wonderful thing I have and provided for me beyond anything I could ever imagine.

He is also the One with whom I have a deep and personal relationship, the One who has completely changed my life, and the One I pray will change yours. He keeps me walking in gratitude every moment I breathe, continues not only to give me hope but to increase it, and has taught me more than I could ever comprehend. He originated every good thing in my life, created my intellect, and molded and shaped me into the man I am today.

He is the God without whom I would be nothing, the true and living God, the One who gave His only Son to live a perfect life, to die, and to rise again for my salvation. Amen.

To My Family

I want to begin by thanking God Almighty for the beautiful heritage He gave me in my amazing family. As a child, my siblings and I experienced the best childhood anyone could ask for, which came at a great cost. That cost began in Egypt, where my mother and father were born and raised by parents deeply dedicated to their relationship with God. My father's father pastored in Egypt for sixty-five years. He prayed every single day that someone from his bloodline would become a pastor. I am the answer to those faithful and consistent prayers, that God Himself provided. Almost to the day my grandfather went to be with the LORD, I began serving in ministry. My other grandfather pastored in Egypt for thirty-five years, until he closed his eyes while ministering and opened them in heaven. These remarkable men were married to equally remarkable women, my grandmothers, whose love and nurture gave rise to the godliness my parents walked in.

Thank you to my parents, Samuel and Elaine, who served the Lord long before I was born and who lived with consistent, genuine, and real faith. My greatest discipleship came from them, and I am forever grateful.

My grandparents and my parents are now with the LORD, and I truly desire that they could have seen the day I was able to write about the soon coming of Christ.

A special thanks to my beautiful Aunt Amal, the last living sibling of my mother. She has played a major role not only in my upbringing, but in shaping the man I am today. You are one of the most precious people in my life.

Thank you to my siblings John, Joseph and Jane, each of whom has been uniquely consequential to my growth and my very existence. I am deeply grateful for how close we are and the encouragement we consistently give each other.

A very special thank you to my precious bride Nicole, who showed me in a new and powerful way what it means to experience God's love. She exemplifies the truth declared in the book of Ephesians, that God is able to do exceeding abundantly above all that we ask or think. She is living proof that His goodness goes far beyond anything I ever imagined for my life. Her faithful devotion to our home and nurturing our children is the single reason I'm able to fulfill God's calling my life as a husband, father, pastor, and author. Nicole, you are God's precious gift to me and to our family, and the work I do would not be possible without you.

And I thank God for my three children, two beautiful daughters and a wonderful son, who inspire me every day to remain faithful to what God has called me to do.

Honoring Charlie and Erika

I want to take this unique opportunity to publicly thank God for the gift of two very special people in my life, Charlie and Erika Kirk. Watching them grow in the grace of God has been one of the greatest experiences of my life. When my little brother Charlie was tragically martyred, the heartbreak in that moment gave way to hearing some of the most inspiring words ever spoken to me. As I sat with his widow Erika, she looked at me with deep conviction and said that more than ever she wanted to know more about Bible prophecy and heaven because she longed to be reunited with her Charlie once again. She went on to express how important it was for her to carry the legacy God entrusted to her, not just for her precious children but in obedience to the God of heaven who called her.

This book reflects the hope that comes from observing a life of obedience to biblical instruction. This is the kind of hope modeled in the race Charlie faithfully ran and in the extraordinary way Erika continues to run with strength, determination, faithfulness, and grace.

Erika, the way you live embodies the powerful truth we hold as believers…**the best is yet to come**.

Contents

Introduction i

CHAPTER ONE
The Unveiling of Jesus Christ 1

CHAPTER TWO
Truth Without Love and Love Without Truth 21

CHAPTER THREE
A Church in Crisis 45

CHAPTER FOUR
What Happens After the Rapture 73

CHAPTER FIVE
Who Is Worthy? 95

CHAPTER SIX
The First Four Seals 111

CHAPTER SEVEN
The 144,000 and the Multitude 133

CHAPTER EIGHT
Silence in Heaven 157

CHAPTER NINE
Trumpets of Terror 181

CHAPTER TEN
A Bitter-Sweet Scroll 197

Conclusion 217

Author's Note 231

Introduction

Revelation means exactly what it implies, a *revealing*. In Greek the word for revelation is *apokalypsis* (ἀποκάλυψις). When people talk about the apocalypse, they often picture some ominous moment or zombie-like catastrophe. But the Greek word apokalypsis means exactly what the title suggests: it's a revealing.

When we study the End Times, we see God revealing through His Word exactly what will happen in the future. There are several important things to understand about the Book of Revelation, and these principles apply to our understanding of Israel as well.

The Book of Revelation doesn't present entirely new concepts or truths never heard before. Again, this is why it's called revelation: it's not revealing new insights God has never given. What's being revealed are things we already encountered in the Old Testament.

That's precisely why I once took my congregation through the entire Bible in twenty weeks before approaching Revelation. I knew that before teaching through this book, even before giving an introduction, I needed to lay the foundation from the Old Testament.

To watch my full teaching series on the Bible, *In The Volume Of The Book*, scan the QR code:

This principle becomes clear when we look at John 1:1, "In the beginning was the Word, and the Word was with God, and the Word was God." John continues in verse 14: "And the Word became flesh and dwelt among us." A few verses later, we read: "The law was given by Moses, but grace and truth came through Jesus Christ."

In the original language, John tells us that the law was given by Moses, and grace and truth were realized in that law through Jesus Christ. The coming of Christ and the manifestation of everything we know Him to be, was essentially a revelation. It's a revealing of what the Old Testament had already given us. Jesus Himself was the living Word.

This is a crucial principle: God did not and does not invalidate the Old Testament. The Old Testament remains powerful and authoritative. Rather, Christ validates the Old Testament and fulfills it. Jesus said, "I did not come to destroy the law but to fulfill it, every jot and tittle."

This becomes even more important when we consider even basic doctrines like salvation. I recently watched a religious debate hosted by podcaster Pat Bet-David, where two Christians and two Muslims discussing truth and communication. The exchange was deeply troubling for anyone familiar with Scripture.

The Muslims made several shocking statements: they openly endorsed Sharia law and said they had no problem with Allah's command to kill infidels. When the Christians were questioned about their beliefs concerning non-believers, the Muslims challenged them on Old Testament passages where God ordered the extermination of entire peoples, asking how this differed from Quranic violence.

The Christians made a critical error by claiming that "God eliminated the Old Testament" and that "the Old Testament doesn't matter." The Muslims, like any skilled debaters, immediately pressed them: how do Christians decide which parts of the Bible are valid and which aren't? They pointed out that Muslims, by contrast, consider the entire Quran authoritative. These Christians lost the debate badly because they failed to accurately represent what the Bible actually teaches.

The correct response should have been: "You're absolutely right. The verses you're quoting create a serious problem for anyone who commits sin. Unlike what you might read in the Quran, the Bible says that the wages of sin include not only physical death but eternal death. So you don't just die as a result of pagan behavior and evil, you'll be condemned to death forever. You'll go to hell for eternity."

We don't throw away the Old Testament or treat it as invalid. The key difference between the Quran and our Old Testament is that ours is real and true, proclaiming truth, while the Quran proclaims lies.

In the Quran, the false god Allah, which the Quran says is

the chief of liars, requires people to sacrifice their sons and themselves so they can take over the world.

But the truth we receive from the Bible is astonishing, and it secures Christ's authority: The one true God never required us to sacrifice ourselves or our children. Instead, God sacrificed His Son, Jesus.

Why? Because in the Old Testament, the blood of a spotless lamb was required to atone for sins. Jesus, called the Lamb of God, fulfilled this requirement by living a sinless life and dying for our sins on the cross. His fulfillment of the Old Testament gives Him the authority to forgive our sin. Instead of us facing the consequences the Old Testament prescribed, Jesus came to earth, lived the perfect life and bore the full weight of sin and death so we wouldn't have to.

Understanding Revelation's Purpose

The Book of Revelation doesn't give us permission to invent new doctrines based on wild speculation. Yet many people create crazy teachings based on what they read in Revelation. Some claim the Antichrist is artificial intelligence. This simply isn't true. While he might use AI to accomplish what we read about in Revelation Chapter 13, the Antichrist himself is not artificial intelligence. He will be a sophisticated, uniquely powerful man who will do evil things. We know this because the Bible tells us he is a man who will be possessed by the devil. The Old Testament reveals who this man is long before the Book of Revelation ever discusses him.

You need to know the Old Testament because once you understand it, Revelation becomes exactly what it claims to be, an apocalypse, a revealing of things that have already been communicated to us. We can understand what the Word says about the coming time because those foundations were established in the Old Testament first.

What's particularly important about the Book of Revelation is that it addresses themes the Old Testament explores throughout, events that are coming to pass. When we read about the Mark of the Beast in Revelation Chapter 13, we learn about a mark that everyone will be forced to take, a wicked beast, and all the unrighteousness that will follow. Scripture gives us insight into who this beast will be. We aren't given the identity of the specific man, but we learn that the beast will essentially be Satan possessing and working through a person raised up in that moment.

If you read and understand the Book of Daniel before diving into Revelation, you'll discover that Daniel lays out nearly everything you'll read about in Revelation. When you come across the seals, trumpets, and different judgments, it all clicks into place. The Bible already tells us these things would happen.

When we examine current events, we need to remember that things aren't falling apart. They're falling into place, coming together exactly as prophesied.

Events in Israel

I experienced this reality firsthand. I have an app on my device that alerts me every time a rocket is launched into Israel. The notifications had become so frequent that I'd almost muted them. Hamas and Hezbollah, both Iranian proxies, attack Israel regularly. Some people mistakenly question whether Hamas, a Sunni organization, could truly serve as a proxy for Shiite Iran. Hamas indeed, operates as Iran's proxy because both share the same goal: Israel's destruction. Hamas' charter explicitly calls for the elimination of the Jewish state and all Jews worldwide.

On October 7, 2023, I started seeing an unusual number of rocket attack notifications, about a hundred in a span of 30-40 minutes, targeting Jerusalem and Tel Aviv. And then my friend David Tal texted me: "James, pray for us. It's bad."

David lives in Modi'in, about thirty miles from most of the fighting in Judea and Samaria and roughly twenty miles southeast of Tel Aviv. Whenever missiles are fired toward Tel Aviv or Jerusalem, the rockets and the Iron Dome interceptors streak right over his home. He told me the night sky was lit up with explosions.

As we talked over the next hour and a half, it became clear that this might be one of the darkest days in Israel's history. Most people don't understand that, largely because they're not getting honest reporting. Many in the media, Fox News included, simply say "fighting in Gaza" without revealing the sheer viciousness of these attacks.

What unfolded across Israel was staggering. Scores of Palestinian men, specifically Hamas operatives, were used by the devil in unprecedented ways. The missile barrage we were watching was nothing more than a diversion. While thousands of rockets rained down to distract the Jewish people, armed Hamas terrorists swept into Israeli neighborhoods and Jewish communities, murdering civilians, injuring thousands, taking hostages, and even parasailing into residential areas. It was an unthinkably brutal act of war.

David described it as "our 9/11, a hundred times worse." Those were difficult words to hear from a Jew whose people have endured tremendous historical tragedies.

Some people have speculated the events of October 7 contradict Bible prophecy because certain teachers have long spoken of an initial season of peace in the land. In truth, what happened aligns seamlessly with that prophetic picture. However, the upheaval Israel experienced will only strengthen the resolve of its people to defend their homeland and take whatever measures are necessary to ensure their safety.

We've never seen Israelis enter Palestinian homes to rob, kill, or destroy. Despite what some in the media claim, Israel doesn't do that. In fact, many Israeli Defense Force casualties over the past decade have occurred while they were protecting innocent Palestinian families.

David shared a story about leading his tank regiment into a city where they were under fire, only to discover that Palestinians had taken over an innocent family's home and were shooting from inside. Their goal was for the tank to return fire, destroy the house, and kill the civilians inside so they could later claim that Israel had targeted innocent people. It revealed their true motive; they had no regard for civilians or human life.

What we're seeing, both then and now, is exactly what the Bible said would happen. This is the foundation I need you to understand as we dive into the Book of Revelation: the Bible is real, the Bible is true, and what we read in Revelation describes events that will unfold in the future.

Revelation isn't just a list of events the Bible predicted

long before the book was written, it also gives us a detailed and descriptive picture of what John actually saw. God used several methods to speak to John as he wrote. First, the LORD spoke to John directly. God also sent an angel, a messenger, who showed him these things. We know John relied on the Word of God, and then the LORD Himself held John's hand, enabling him to see the future.

John begins:

> "The revelation of Jesus Christ, which God gave unto him to show unto his servants things which must shortly come to pass; and He sent and signified it by his angel unto his servant John."

Revelation 1:1

Notice that many Bibles call the last book "The Revelation of Saint John the Divine", a title given by man. But the Bible tells us the correct title right there in Revelation 1:1. It says, "The revelation of Jesus Christ."

We read that God sent angels to speak to John throughout Revelation, but in Chapter 1, Christ Himself delivers the message God is giving and reveals the vision God allows John to see. John receives an extraordinary opportunity to witness events far beyond his lifetime. He writes this around 96 A.D., while exiled on the island of Patmos.

The story of how he came to be on this island is remarkable. His persecutors actually tried to kill him by throwing him into a boiling pot of oil, intending to fry him alive, but it didn't harm him at all. Unable to kill him, they exiled him to the island of Patmos instead. It's striking how God transformed this exile into an opportunity, using it to give John the greatest work and deepest insight he'd ever receive: the Book of Revelation. The text also tells us: "Who bore record of the Word of God, and of the testimony of Jesus Christ, and of all things that he saw."

The Promise of Blessing

Here's a point I need to emphasize because it's so important. Make a note on this page, this should be a major focus not only for this Introduction but for every single day you spend studying this book.

> "Blessed is he that readeth, and they that hear the words of this prophecy, and keep those things which are written therein: for the time is at hand."

Revelation 1:3

I love that the phrase "the time is at hand" resonates more powerfully with us today than ever before. The Bible promises blessings not just from reading the Book of Revelation, but from hearing it as well. Simply by listening to teaching on Revelation, God will bless you.

I tell pastors all the time: "If you want to learn how to grow your church, make Revelation one of the first books you teach." Many push back, saying it's too hard to understand or teach, which is just one of the many misconceptions about the Book of Revelation. Some pastors even believe that teaching or reading Revelation will lead to demon possession. I'm not kidding. They really think you'll become demon-possessed because of strange traditions passed down over generations. The enemy wants to put up every possible roadblock to keep people from reading Revelation, and he does it through lies and misconceptions like these.

But Revelation is the only book in the Bible that makes this kind of promise, a blessing for reading it. Whether you hear the Book of Revelation being read, hear it being taught, or read and study it yourself, the Bible says you'll be blessed as a result.

I can't think of a better way to open this Introduction than by highlighting the promise, that God will bless you for studying the Book of Revelation. So don't be surprised when, as we work through this book together, you find yourself blessed beyond belief.

With that in mind, we're going to focus on Revelation Chapters 1 through 10 in this book.

By the end of Revelation Chapter 10, the first major movement of the book reaches its climax. Christ has been revealed in His glory, the churches have been addressed, the heavenly throne room has been unveiled, six seals have been opened, six trumpets have sounded, and the world has been plunged into unprecedented judgment. And still, mankind refuses to repent. At this point, there's an interlude of judgment and Jesus reaffirms His authority, recommissions John, and announces that the long-promised "mystery of God" is about to be completed. This moment creates the hinge of the entire book, setting the stage for the events that unfold in Chapters 11–22 which will be covered in my next book.

The Key to Understanding Revelation

Here's the other thing you need to know, and it's critical: There's a key to understanding Revelation. One verse in particular reveals the timeline of the entire book. You have to know this verse. Without it, you'll struggle to follow what happens when.

Jesus makes it crystal clear. He tells John:

"Write the things which thou hast seen, and the things which are, and the things which shall be hereafter."

Revelation 1:19

Let me break this down for you, because I can show you exactly how this maps to different sections of Revelation. John is given three distinct categories to write about:

The things which you have seen: Revelation Chapter 1. When Jesus tells John to write the things that he has seen, it's Chapter 1.

The things which are: This means the current day, the day that we're in right now. That's Revelation Chapters 2 and 3. We'll talk about the Church Age and what it means and why that's such a valuable thing.

The things which are to come: This is the rest of the book, starting in Revelation Chapter 4 and going straight through the end. If you can see the structure of the Book of Revelation this way, the entire book becomes much easier to understand.

The Three-Part Structure Explained

Let me give you a perfect example. In Chapter 1, as John writes about what he has seen, he's bearing witness to what happened to him and what drove him to write about both present and future events. What does John see? He gives us a description of Jesus, who appeared to him. We'll dive deep into that.

Then he talks about the things which are, Chapters 2 and 3. He writes seven letters to seven churches, dictated by Jesus Himself. Jesus instructs, "Write these words down to the pastors of the churches." Each church receives a specific message, and every one of those messages still applies to us today. Every single one. They describe a time period that hasn't ended yet. Revelation Chapters 2 and 3 cover the time leading up to when the church is raptured. Once the church is raptured, we move directly into Revelation Chapter 4. It's crucial that you make that connection now.

What's going to excite you as you study the Book of Revelation is how it clearly illustrates real time events and patterns we're observing in the world today.

We're going to walk through the seven letters to the seven churches. After that, we'll move into Chapter 4, where John describes God's throne, a really key passage. In Chapters 3 and 4, we'll discuss why the rapture happens.

Chapter 5 serves as a prelude that leads us into the seven seals. We'll examine how these transitions work. Throughout Revelation, we have the seal judgments, the trumpet judgments, and the bowl judgments. Before each new set of judgments begins, there's a prelude. This pattern is crucial to recognize because it's going to help you understand how God consistently works throughout Scripture.

If you're familiar with the Old Testament, you'll immediately see the connection. You'll think, "Oh, wow, I've seen this pattern before."

The Geopolitical Key

Revelation Chapter 6, is the greatest reason I make this argument: all pastors should be the best geopolitical analysts in the world. We should know politics and government better than anyone alive.

Why? Because the Bible reveals the heart, mindset and thinking behind human governments. Every form of government ever known to man appears in the Bible in one way or another. These include patriarchal (family-based), theocratic (God-ruled), monarchal (kings), totalitarian, communist, and socialist systems.

I can even show you how the United States, a democratic republic, is built on a biblical foundation. Many of our laws were shaped by precedents found in the Bible.

To prove this point further, study the Bible more deeply than you ever have before. Then read *The Federalist Papers*, and you'll quickly understand the founding fathers' mindset and what motivated them to draft laws the way they did. William Federer, and important figure in the body of Christ and, in my opinion, the greatest American historian alive, shows you exactly where biblical precedent was established in the writing of both the Declaration of Independence and the Constitution.

Revelation Chapter 6 shows us exactly what happens under totalitarian rule. What many miss is this pattern of totalitarianism traces directly back to the fallout of Adam's sin.

Revelation Chapter 6 even describes the patterns we're seeing in situations like Ukraine right now. You've probably heard the quote: "Power tends to corrupt and absolute power corrupts absolutely." That idea makes complete sense when we apply it to what's happening in the world today.

We'll examine the rider of the white horse, in this case, the Antichrist, and see how he mirrors the historical totalitarian rulers we've known.

Next comes the rider of the red horse, who represents war. Totalitarian rule always brings war with it.

Then the rider of the black horse brings economic failure and collapse, the third seal described in Revelation Chapter 6.

So the pattern unfolds: a totalitarian ruler comes into power and brings war. Following war is economic failure.

The third seal includes a striking warning: "Do not touch the oil and the wine," which is another way of saying, don't interfere with the ruling class. These are the people who run the war machine and uphold the totalitarian order. Does that sound familiar? Think of people like George Soros, Bill Gates, the Clintons, and others.

The fourth seal reveals a grim picture: a rider on a pale horse who brings death. We're seeing this pattern unfold before our eyes today.

Spoiler alert: I am going to mention the mark of the beast, which appears later in Revelation Chapters 13 and 14. I bring it up because a lot of people assume that those who take the mark will be forced into it. I've even heard people say, "Well, if the rapture happens and I'm left behind, I just won't take the mark." But that's not what the Bible teaches. Scripture shows they'll take it willingly. And even then, God sends an angel in Revelation Chapter 14 pleading with them, "Don't do this, whatever you do, don't take this mark," because the consequences are eternal. Yet despite that clear warning, people still won't listen.

The Final Battle and a 200 Million Army

As we look at Revelation 9:16, I'm going to clear up a common misconception about the 200 million army.

Consider the war that happened on Yom Kippur. Israel won that battle because Syria failed to account for the logistics needed to move a massive armory into the Golan Heights. I know a man who served in a tank regiment in the Golan Heights on Yom Kippur. His regiment spotted enemy tanks coming over the hill. They were stunned to see rows and rows of enemy tanks stretching before them. The soldiers in his regiment basically told each other, "We're dead. Prepare yourselves. We're going to die on Yom Kippur. There's no hope."

Then suddenly, as they prepared to engage, all the enemy tanks stopped, almost as if to say, "Come get us. We want to be destroyed." The Israeli soldiers quickly recognized their opportunity to strike, and destroyed the entire enemy regiment. Why did those tanks suddenly stop in their tracks? Simple: Syria hadn't accounted for the fuel needed to keep their tanks running. It was amazing to witness, and Israel won the war.

My point is this: there's no way you can transport 200 million human beings and all their necessary equipment into what Revelation describes as the final battle. The army in Revelation 9:16 isn't a traditional human force, and I'll explain why. As we go through this, you'll see the differences between what's mostly a literal description of future events and what's specifically metaphorical.

A Promise and Call to Action

We're watching the spiritual seasons shift, just like when autumn arrives and the leaves change colors. Look at what's unfolding in Israel right now. These world events are setting the stage for the "main event."

Here's how to think about it: When we start seeing signs of the tribulation we know is coming, when things we read about in the Book of Revelation begin to happen, we know the rapture is near. Why? Because the rapture has to happen before everything else does.

And friends, we're getting there. We are so close to that time. Christ's return could come at any moment. Let's wake up. God is real and His Word is true. I make you this promise: Your life will be radically changed as you study the Book of Revelation.

1
The Unveiling of Jesus Christ

For many people, the Book of Revelation is hard to understand and, yes, even scary. But it doesn't have to be. If you've felt intimidated by this final book of the Bible, I want to change that perspective completely. What I'm going to share with you is an incredible tool that will give you clarity about what Revelation says and remove any confusion from your mind about what God intended for us to understand when we read this book.

This has always been difficult for a lot of people, for many different reasons. I've heard every kind of crazy thing imaginable. I've heard people tell me that if they read the Book of Revelation, they're going to have a curse put on them. I've heard people say they just can't understand it because it's too far out, too many weird things. I hear lots of other explanations that are, in my opinion, very far fetched.

But in reality, I don't blame people for having these feelings, because the things they are told constantly about this book bring about confusion, mysticism, and strange ideas about something the Bible actually wants to make simple and clear.

The truth is, there's so much controversy centered around this book, and it's been especially interesting lately. You have popular figures making statements about Revelation that are terribly incorrect. And of course, one of the greatest problems within Bible study at any level is when people tend to apply everything as some kind of allegorical or metaphorical event, when I don't believe God intended for us to look at the Bible that way.

Don't get me wrong (there are times where we do see types, and there are times where we see metaphors. There are times where we see something that might be uniquely allegorical within a particular context, but that is not the Bible in general.) The Bible is a very accurate historical document. It's a powerful, enriching tool, and it is the source of life. It is quite literal and is intended to be taken literally.

The True Meaning of "Revelation"

Revelation comes from the Greek word *apokalypsis* (ἀποκάλυψις), which means "the revealing." So immediately, we need to understand that the Book of Revelation was not written to cause mystery and confusion. The Book of Revelation was designed to bring clarity and to reveal something that might not be easily understood otherwise.

This is powerful when you think about it. God designed the Book of Revelation to reveal everything He wants us to know, especially connecting so much of what we see in the Old Testament. And that's why it's really critical if you want to understand the Book of Revelation, you need to know the Old Testament. Not a partial understanding of it, but a complete, whole-counsel-of-God's-Word understanding.

So many people in Bible prophecy do such a terrible job teaching passages like this. Teaching Revelation requires an in-depth understanding of everything in the Old Testament. If you don't have that understanding, or you have a limited, localized understanding, then you're not going to recognize the greater and more specific issues that God wants us to understand, and you're going to come to some really bad conclusions.

This is why we see people in the Bible prophecy world teaching all kinds of crazy things (setting dates for the rapture, creating allegories you wouldn't believe. The problem starts when people miss the overall context of the Bible. Without that foundation, they come to very bad conclusions.

The Author and the Authority

Let's jump right into the text. We'll start with verse one, written by the apostle John when he was in his nineties. There had been multiple attempts made on his life because of the impact he had and his message of the Gospel. Some of the most impacting words he had ever written were in the Gospel According to John, which started with that beautiful picture of Christ being the Living Word.

After these multiple attempts on his life, he ended up on the island of Patmos, where he was exiled. You would think that after something like that, your life would be over (that would be the end of the game). But in reality, the most significant document ever written by the apostle John would be written on that island. The depth of insight it provides is life-changing on so many levels.

"The revelation of Jesus Christ, which God gave unto him, to shew unto his servants things which must shortly come to pass; and He sent and signified it by his angel unto his servant John."

Revelation 1:1

Right away, the first verse tells you so much of what you need to know about the premise of the Book of Revelation. There's been a lot of misunderstanding about this. There are countless speculations about the purpose of Revelation, but we have the purpose given to us right here. It's really simple: it is the revealing of Jesus Christ which God gave unto John, to show unto his servants things which must shortly come to pass.

A lot of people say that when we talk about "the revelation of Jesus Christ," it means Christ is being revealed. While Christ is revealed on every page, this is really Christ Himself handing down to us, through John, a revealing of everything we've already learned in the Old Testament and, undoubtedly, in the New.

If you look at it from that perspective, it becomes much bigger than some present being unwrapped with Jesus in the middle of it. Jesus is foundational (the most fundamental part of all this, undoubtedly). But this is Christ, who has already been revealed to us, now handing down a revelation of all of the Word of God. He's revealing to us the things that are going to happen soon.

The Credible Witness

Look at what verse two tells us about John:

> "Who bare record of the Word of God, and of the testimony of Jesus Christ, and of all things that he saw."
>
> **Revelation 1:2**

This is where it gets really important, even in the first two verses. This is Jesus revealing to us things that are shortly going to come to pass (involving our understanding of the culmination of everything we've learned in the Old Testament). He sent and signified it by his angel to John, who was the one who bore record of the Word of God and of the testimony of Jesus Christ, and all things that he saw.

What this is telling you is that John is a credible person to hand this information down because he's already borne record of the Word of God. He's established credentials as the person giving us this message, and God wants us to understand that this message is literal. Why? Because John, who bore record of the Word of God, who bore record of the testimony of Jesus Christ and all the things he saw, is also the one bringing us this information that was signified by the LORD himself concerning the times that are coming.

We have to get this straight from the start because a lot of people say Revelation is mystical and get all weird about it, but it's not that way. If you understand what Jesus is describing it here, it's going to make so much more sense.

The Blessing Promise

Here's something that will blow your mind when you truly understand it. Look at verse three:

> "Blessed is he that readeth, and they that hear the words of this prophecy, and keep those things which

are written therein: for the time is at hand."

Revelation 1:3

Let me make myself really clear here. So many people talk about being scared of the Book of Revelation because of the things it says will happen. They also talk about how difficult it is to understand. I've heard lots of pastors say they've taught every book in the Bible but will not teach through Revelation. They stay away from it. The reason we should study Revelation is right here in verse three.

"Blessed is he that readeth, and they that hear the words of this prophecy, and keep those things which are written therein: for the time is at hand."

Revelation 1:3

In other words, the fastest way to gain immense blessing from the LORD (wonderful blessing from God) is by simply reading through, hearing the words, and putting into practice what you find in the Book of Revelation.

You have an enemy that hates you. You have a devil that absolutely hates your guts. He will do everything he can to keep you away from getting blessing from the LORD, which is specifically why he will make Revelation seem the way it does to so many people. If he can put spiritual blindness in people's eyes, if he can make it all fuzzy language, if he can cause people to make all kinds of bad interpretations, if he can cause it to feel mysterious, well, then he wins. Because the less people study Revelation, the less blessed they'll actually be, and they're never going to get all that God designed for them to have.

So I'm here to tell you what God says: if you want to be blessed in your life, start studying the Book of Revelation. Listen, it doesn't just say "blessed is he that readeth." It says "and they that hear the words of this prophecy." So if you're not someone who's big on reading, you can listen to teaching on Revelation and allow it to minister to you. I promise you will see your life radically change through that process. This is the only book in the Bible that God promises He will bless you specifically for studying it and hearing the words and honoring those words.

The Seven Churches and Seven Spirits

"John to the seven churches which are in Asia: Grace be unto you, and peace from him which is, and which was, and which is to come, and from the seven spirits which are before his throne."

Revelation 1:4

This ties directly back to the Book of Isaiah and several other Old Testament passages. If you want to better understand Revelation, you have to understand the Old Testament in its whole context. When someone with a Jewish background heard these greetings of grace and peace, they understood something profound. Grace (the Greek word *charis* [χάρις], where we get "charisma") means God looks upon you favorably without any merit on your part. He looks upon you favorably even though you might not have any reason to be liked, but God still looks at you that way.

If you don't experience God's grace by accepting it, you will never know what the peace of God means. When they heard *charis* and *shalom*, they understood: receive the unmerited favor God has chosen to bestow upon you, and upon receiving it, you will then experience his peace. You're not going to experience it any other way.

The seven spirits referenced here connect directly to Isaiah chapter 11, where we read about the spirit of the LORD, the spirit of wisdom and understanding, the spirit of counsel and might, the spirit of knowledge and the fear of the LORD. These represent the complete characteristics of God's Spirit working in the life of Christ and, by extension, in believers.

Christ the Faithful Witness

"And from Jesus Christ, who is the faithful witness, the first begotten of the dead, and the prince of the kings of the earth. Unto him that loved us, and washed us from our sins in his own blood."

Revelation 1:5

This brings us to another crucial aspect of understanding Revelation: you're never going to understand it fully if you're not walking with the LORD. If you have put your faith and trust in Jesus Christ and received the gift He has given for salvation, then you are at the first major step to better understand this book, because you need inspiration from the Holy Spirit to confirm the things you're looking at. When we look at Christ being called "the faithful witness," understand something important. In legal terms, when we look at someone who's a faithful witness or a good witness, it means they're giving us accurate depictions of what's actually happening to the point that we have information that's actionable. Jesus is a faithful witness. He is giving us information here in Revelation that is so good, so reliable, so accurate, so perfect that it's actually actionable.

Our Identity in Christ

"And hath made us kings and priests unto God and his Father; to him be glory and dominion for ever and ever. Amen."

Revelation 1:6

So many of us view ourselves in the context of what we do. Our identity becomes what we do instead of who we actually are. This is the problem with the confusion we see in the world today (people being unsure of themselves, not even recognizing basic truth about identity). The Bible says that if you are walking with the LORD (if you are a person who has received the free gift of Christ and said, "LORD, I put my faith and trust in you") then guess what? You're a king and a priest. Your identity is in Christ. And if your identity is in Christ, it changes the way you live.

The Promise of His Coming

"Behold, he cometh with clouds; and every eye shall see him, and they also which pierced him: and all kindreds of the earth shall wail because of him. Even so, Amen."

Revelation 1:7

You might be denying Christ right now, you might not accept him, but one day everyone is going to see him in full and living color. When they do, they're going to weep for the fact that they rejected Him, because rejection of Christ brings torment to a soul forever. Look at the declaration Christ makes in verse eight:

> "I am Alpha and Omega, the beginning and the ending, saith the LORD, which is, and which was, and which is to come, the Almighty."
>
> **Revelation 1:8**

Jesus is not just saying He's the one who started it and the one who ends it. Jesus is saying He's the one who was always there (He existed before, and He will exist after). He's not just the end cap to those time periods, but He is the creator of those time periods. He has always existed before those time periods even existed, before the dimension of physics was even created, before time itself was created. God was there.

John's Vision on Patmos

John explains his situation in verses nine and ten:

> "I John, who also am your brother, and companion in tribulation, and in the kingdom and patience of Jesus Christ, was in the isle that is called Patmos, for the Word of God, and for the testimony of Jesus Christ. I was in the Spirit on the LORD's day, and heard behind me a great voice, as of a trumpet."
>
> **Revelation 1:9–10**

Notice how John identifies himself (not as "the great reverend" or demanding his apostolic title). He simply says, "I am your brother and companion in tribulation." He's one of us, going through this with us, here to tell us everything we need to know about what's happening in the future.

When John says he was "in the Spirit on the LORD's day," he's talking about being filled with the Spirit of God, likely on Sunday. The early church called Sunday "the LORD's Day." Here's valuable insight: when you give a day to the LORD, when you choose to place priority on spiritual things on a specific day, that's often when God will communicate with you the most (not because God chooses to communicate on one day over another, but because when you dedicate time specifically to spiritual things, you allow your mind and heart to be more open to God's voice).

The Glorious Vision of Christ

The voice tells John in verse eleven:

"I am Alpha and Omega, the first and the last: and, What thou seest, write in a book, and send it unto the seven churches which are in Asia; unto Ephesus, and unto Smyrna, and unto Pergamos, and unto Thyatira, and unto Sardis, and unto Philadelphia, and unto Laodicea."

Revelation 1:11

Then comes John's incredible vision of the glorified Christ:

"And I turned to see the voice that spake with me. And being turned, I saw seven golden candlesticks; And in the midst of the seven candlesticks one like unto the Son of man, clothed with a garment down to the foot, and girt about the paps with a golden girdle. His head and his hairs were white like wool, as white as snow; and his eyes were as a flame of fire; And his feet like unto fine brass, as if they burned in a furnace; and his voice as the sound of many waters. And he had in his right hand seven stars: and out of his mouth went a sharp two edged sword: and his countenance was as the sun shineth in his strength."

Revelation 1:12–16

This is very literal. None of this is allegorical. John is seeing something very specific and describing it. If you understand what the Scripture teaches concerning Christ, this description shouldn't surprise you or seem weird, because this is talking about God in a very powerful and glorified state with a very specific purpose.

When we talk about characteristics like brass feet, understand that brass represents judgment. When John looked at Jesus, he recognized Jesus was no joke. The voice like "the sound of many waters" (in ancient cultures, water was the most fearful frontier. When you heard the loud sound of waves roaring, it was very fearful). The whole idea is that when John looked upon Jesus, he recognized Jesus wasn't messing around. He's looking at deity (at God himself).

John's Response to Christ's Glory

"And when I saw him, I fell at His feet as dead. And He laid his right hand upon me, saying unto me, Fear not; I am the first and the last."

Revelation 1:17

I can identify with John. If I saw Christ appear this way, I would probably fall down as dead too. When you have people telling you, "Oh yeah, the LORD appeared to me and I just said, 'Hey, God, what's up?'" (No, it doesn't work that way). If the LORD appears to you, you're going to fall down as dead, realizing Who you're in front of, Almighty God.

But watch what happens. John sees Jesus in this state and faints. The picture I see is the LORD actually leaning down, gently touching him, and saying, "Fear not."

Look at what Jesus says here:

"I am He that liveth, and was dead; and, behold, I am alive for evermore, Amen; and have the keys of hell and of death."

Revelation 1:18

This makes me emotional when I think about it. At one point Jesus was alive. He was crucified. And guess what, He resurrected from the dead and is alive again. He kicked death straight in the teeth, and now we have life because of Him.

When people are fearful about studying Revelation for whatever reason (fearful they won't understand, fearful it'll be confusing, fearful they'll hear something that will scare them), Jesus is commanding, saying, "Don't fear. Why? Because I am the One who's alive. I was dead, and now I'm alive. And behold, I am alive forever. I'm not going anywhere. And I have the keys to hell and death."

If you listen to Him, obey Him, walk with him, He's got the keys. You will experience an eternity of reward and pleasure and joy. The command is: don't be fearful. Don't let anything keep you from studying Revelation, because it contains the blessing of God.

The Key to Understanding Everything

Now we come to the verse I wanted to focus on, because verse nineteen is the key to the Book of Revelation. It's really interesting (I don't think it's a coincidence that in verse eighteen Jesus talks about having the keys of hell and death, and then gives us the key to the Book of Revelation).

> "Write the things which thou hast seen, and the things which are, and the things which shall be hereafter."

Revelation 1:19

If you're taking notes, write this down, because it's important. John is told to write three categories:

Category One: "The things which thou hast seen" (This is Revelation Chapter 1. John was told to write the things that happened that he witnessed in that moment.)

Category Two: "The things which are" (These are the letters Jesus writes to the seven churches, Chapters 2 and 3. The Church Age still is not over, so we are technically living in Revelation Chapters 2 and 3 right now.)

Category Three: "The things which shall be hereafter" (Hereafter what? Hereafter the rapture of the church, hereafter the time when the Church Age is over. The Church Age is over at the very beginning of Revelation Chapter 4. When you see the phrase "after these things," the church gets raptured.

So: Revelation Chapter 1 = things John has seen. Revelation Chapters 2 and 3 = things which are. Revelation Chapters

4 through 22 = things which shall be hereafter. Three categories. Very simple.

Here's what I need everyone to understand: if you apply your understanding of Revelation using these categories, it becomes so much easier. You'll hear people say, "Well, the church is going to be around during this time," or pastors giving messages saying, "When the mark of the beast comes your way, don't accept it." That's a great message, but that message is not for the church, because the church will not be here during that time.

There are so many things you can learn by simply understanding the timeline. If you know the timeline and understand how the book is organized based on what God tells us in Revelation 1:19, you'll never be confused. When you're studying something in Revelation Chapter 4 and after, you don't have to worry about being on earth during that time because you know you're gone by Chapter 4.

Understanding that timeline helps you understand so much more and gives you a better foundation for what you're seeing.

Essential Guidelines for Study

Let me give you a couple of pieces of advice with all this knowledge.

First, always view Revelation as literal. Do not fall into the trap that says John was living during a time when he didn't understand what he was seeing, so of course he'd say "scorpion" if he was looking at a helicopter. Don't take on that mindset, because when that mindset is taken, people make lots of mistakes.

The Word of God is powerful on so many levels because it was inspired by God. It is His Word. He gave it to man. I believe God would have inspired John to write using terminology that would alert us if everything was metaphorical, and he was describing something he'd never seen before. But that's not what's going on.

Yes, undoubtedly John was seeing things he'd never seen before, but I believe he was seeing things in the spiritual realm. We make terrible mistakes when we over spiritualize. For example, there's massive confusion between Revelation Chapters 9 and 16. Because of that confusion, people think there's this human army coming out of China. That's not the case, and we'll look at what the real answer is later.

There are several of places in Revelation where people get very metaphorical or allegorical when God never intended that to be the case. In every avenue possible, seek to look at it literally.

Second, spend as much time as possible understanding and knowing the Old Testament. Even if it means putting yourself on a schedule, reading through the Old Testament, seeking to understand it (know the stories, go through the Old Testament, and don't skip anything). The more you know the Old Testament, the better you become at understanding Revelation. And the better you become at understanding Bible prophecy.

The Mystery Revealed

Finally, for those who might not know what the seven stars

and seven candlesticks are, you don't have to listen to speculation, because Jesus gives you the answer in verse twenty:

> "The mystery of the seven stars which thou sawest in my right hand, and the seven golden candlesticks. The seven stars are the angels of the seven churches: and the seven candlesticks which thou sawest are the seven churches."
>
> **Revelation 1:20**

Remember that word "mystery" (information you would never know unless it was revealed to you). It's like when my daughter does something we'd never see, then something inside her convicts her and she comes to us and says, "Mama, I did this." That's the biblical definition of mystery (information we would never know unless she revealed it to us).

The seven candlesticks represent the church, the body of Christ. The seven stars are the messengers of the churches (*angelos* means "the messenger"), the pastors of the churches. If you are a pastor, a true messenger to the Church of Jesus Christ, you are one of those stars in the hand of God.

This is important for pastors to know: That's a twofold thing. First, it's a blessing (being in the hand of God means He holds you and will protect you as the messenger of the church). But it also means He can discipline you if you choose to take advantage of that position. That's the faithfulness of God.

Ready for What's Coming

This is why I've never really been concerned about the consequences of speaking truth. I'm going to bring the message God has asked me to bring, regardless of the consequences. Why? Because I'm in the hand of God, and Christ is walking in the midst of the body. There can be no more powerful picture than that.

This brings us into the seven letters to the seven churches, and I can promise you, if you've never walked through those letters, it's going to change your life. You're going to be blown away. Get ready to experience some of the greatest spiritual growth you've ever experienced as we go through these letters, because the insight given is going to be amazing.

Get ready to be confronted. Get ready to be rebuked. Get ready to be blessed. Get ready to be encouraged. It's all going to happen, and your minds are going to be blown by everything being communicated.

The Book of Revelation isn't something to fear (it's something to embrace). God promises to bless you for studying it. He's given you the key to understanding it. And He's revealed Himself in power and glory to show you that no matter what's coming, He holds all things in His hands.

We are the church. We should be the ones with the answers, and we shouldn't be confused. We should know what the Bible says. These are the tools that will help you better understand not just Revelation, but your walk with God. There's so much more there, but these are the foundations, and you'll be blessed as a result.

2

Truth Without Love and Love Without Truth

We are rapidly approaching the end. We see things happening around us that are not only unprecedented but continue to serve as evidence that we are approaching the time that God's Word promised us we would one day be facing. It's extraordinary because we are living in an absolutely remarkable time, definitely something the world has never seen before. Every day I wake up and see something new, something that I haven't seen before, and it's mind-boggling. With the advent of AI and other crazy things going on, things are changing so rapidly, we can't even keep track of it. But as I've said before, we knew this would happen.

One part of understanding the time we are living in and recognizing that we are indeed in the last days is being aware of the warnings God gives us regarding the things we should expect. So the place we need to look to is the book of Revelation, specifically, the letters Jesus wrote to the seven churches.

Living in the Church Age

Before we dive into these powerful letters, let me remind

you of something critical: we are currently living in what Revelation calls "the things which are," the Church Age. We have not yet seen the beginning of Revelation Chapter 4. We are technically living in Revelation Chapters 2 and 3 right now. Although each church represents a specific time period historically, all of them apply to us in our current age. How do we know? Because Jesus says at the end of each letter, "He that hath an ear, let him hear what the spirit saith unto the churches." If you have an ear to hear, then these letters are written directly to you and me.

These messages are more relevant today than they've ever been. Why? Because we're living in the last days and the stakes are getting higher. The warnings are designed to give us direction and insight concerning how we live and the life that is to come.

Keeping these very important things in mind, allow me to state the obvious. When God wants His people to live a certain way, what does He do? He tells the pastors to do it first. Those who are called to shepherd and minister to the church, myself included, are called to live in the specific way God wants to see the rest of His people live. God's example is never "do as I say and not as I do." Rather, it is "do as I say and do as I do." When the LORD wants the Body of Christ to behave a specific way, He immediately goes to the pastors and says, "This is what I require of you. This is the obligation set forth. This is how we move in order to see the rest of the Body of Christ move."

This is why I'm full of energy when I teach, because I'm excited about this stuff. I know God's Word is true and I understand the responsibility. I know it's what gives us the power to change our lives and, dare I say, our eternal destinies.

My message to pastors: You must live as the example so the Body of Christ can see you and imitate you.

The Pattern of the Letters

As we look at the seven letters, there's a pattern worth noting. First, Jesus recognizes something good that's happening within each church (except Laodicea). He talks about their works and calls out the admirable things they're doing, and then He gives them a rebuke for what they need to change. Only two churches receive no rebuke: Smyrna and Philadelphia. After pointing out what they're doing right and wrong, in most cases, Jesus provides them with a solution:

- This is what you need to repent of
- This is where you need to go
- And this is how you need to do it

The letters to each of the churches mentioned in Revelation can stir something in our hearts and minds we need to work on or be encouraged with. So it's important we study and understand.

Ephesus: The Church That Left Its First Love

"Unto the angel of the church of Ephesus write; These things saith He that holdeth the seven stars in his right hand, who walketh in the midst of the seven golden candlesticks;"

Revelation 2:1

Some people wonder what Jesus is talking about when He

mentions stars and candlesticks. We don't have to wonder; Jesus tells us exactly what they are in Revelation chapter one:

> "The seven stars are the angels of the seven churches: and the seven candlesticks which thou sawest are the seven churches."
>
> **Revelation 1:20**

The angels are the pastors of the churches. The candlesticks are the churches themselves. So Jesus is saying, "I hold the pastors of the churches in my right hand while I walk in the midst of the church." This is both encouraging and sobering for pastors. It means God protects us as we communicate the message He's called us to communicate. But it also means if we mess around with God's children, He might just crush us. There are great consequences for taking advantage of the role and position God has given. And for the congregation, this message is incredibly encouraging: Jesus is walking in the midst of the church. We're not alone. He's with us, sustaining us, leading us, guiding us.

The Commendations

Look at what Jesus says about Ephesus:

> "I know thy works, and thy labour, and thy patience, and how thou canst not bear them which are evil: and thou hast tried them which say they are apostles, and are not, and hast found them liars: And hast borne, and hast patience, and for my name's sake hast laboured, and hast not fainted."
>
> **Revelation 2:2-3**

So far, it sounds like the church in Ephesus was doing well. They were hardworking, not lazy. They had patience and consistency. They couldn't stand evil and wouldn't tolerate it in their midst. They tested false teachers and exposed them as liars. They endured persecution for Christ's name and didn't give up. This church was blessed with some of the greatest leaders who ever existed. Timothy spent time in Ephesus. John the Apostle was a respected elder there. They were among remarkable people who stood for the truth. They were doing all the right things, working hard, standing against evil, and persevering through trials.

This reminds me a lot like the Conservative Movement today. One could say, "I know your works, I know your labor. I see the patience you've developed. You don't tolerate those who do evil. You have tested those who claim they are good leaders and made it known when you have found them to actually be liars." There are many in today's Conservative Movement who have borne good fruit; they show patience and faithfulness and they even do it in the name of Christ. They work hard and they won't back down.

The Devastating Rebuke

But then comes the heartbreaking condemnation:

"Nevertheless, I have somewhat against thee, because thou hast left thy first love."

Revelation 2:4

Notice Jesus didn't say they *lost* their first love. He said they *left* their first love. They walked away. It wasn't something that happened to them; it was a conscious decision.

How many of us do this? If you've been married more than a few years, you know what I'm talking about. Remember how wonderful you were before you married your spouse? You were kind, thoughtful, patient, and selfless. You thought about all the ways you could bless your future husband or wife. The passion and feelings of love were sometimes overwhelming.

But what happens after you get married and time goes by? Life happens. You have children, your career requires more time and focus, pressures come, and countless things demand your attention and energy. A godly spouse continues to invest in their marriage and labors in the things they know need to be done: raising their children in the ways of the LORD and doing all the things needed to maintain a healthy family life. Except it's very easy to choose other things instead of our first love and we sometimes forget what was special in the beginning. It can start to feel like work, a duty, or just a contractual relationship.

These believers who once were so in love with Jesus got so busy doing things for the LORD, they completely neglected important aspects of their relationship with Him. They walked away from what drew them to Him in the beginning and left the first love.

I know what it's like to labor twenty-plus hours a day in the ministry, getting so caught up in the work that I forget about who I was doing it for. It's easy for us to leave our first love, even using the excuse of ministry work.

This happens in other ways too. Looking at the problems that have occurred in the Conservative Movement, we see what it looks like when leaders adapt to what we call "cultural Christianity." They appear to be doing good things, but they have not been born again and experienced regeneration of their hearts. They are living in the same way Nicodemus did. Maybe they're doing what's right because it's expected or popular. But without being born again and walking with the LORD, they only appear to have a form of godliness. They're actually powerless.

Revelation addresses the church, though. What Jesus is saying is, "You started this work with a deep-rooted love for me, and that deep-rooted love drove you to laboring in my name. You have patience, you do not tolerate those who do evil, and you test those who claim to be true apostles. You are the church of great works. Yet, in the busyness of all you're doing, you have made a conscious decision to walk away from your very first love. You traded what captivated you in the first place, God's love for you, for just doing good things."

How This Applies to Us Personally

Do you remember the time when Jesus became the LORD of your life? He renewed your heart and refreshed your soul. His presence was so real. And because you received Him in your heart and He confirmed everything you believed to be true, it transformed you. The love you reciprocated to Him was substantial. You chose to give your life to Him. You chose to say, "LORD, I'm going to walk with you and I'm going to serve you because of what you've done for me. You're an amazing God."

But perhaps the busyness of doing works for God began to preoccupy you, and it seemed as if you were just going through the motions. Following Him can become routine and you can forget about the love that drove you to Him in the first place.

As a father, I've found myself having to go back to this exercise at times. I could get so caught up in training my children, telling them "no, you've got to follow these rules" and "here are the consequences of disobedience." Sometimes, I've gotten so involved in the process of raising my children that I've had to remind myself to just love them. In that moment, I make a conscious choice to never allow myself to drift from that love.

I often take time to just look at my children, without saying or doing anything, and I'm reminded of how they were an answer to prayer. I think about what makes each of them so special and priceless, and I reflect upon the love that I have for them as their father.

In the same way, sometimes we get so caught up being a child of the King, it's easy to focus on the doing and we lose sight of simply being loved by God.

The Solution: The Three Rs

Jesus gives the church in Ephesus the solution to this problem in verse five. I call it **The Three Rs:**

> "Remember therefore from whence thou art fallen, and repent, and do the first works; or else I will come unto thee quickly, and remove thy candlestick out of his place, except thou repent."

Revelation 2:5

The First "R" is Remember

Take a moment to pause and remember the very beginning, the first days. Jesus isn't asking you to do the exact same things you did in the beginning; He's asking you to remember the heart and mind that drove you to those actions. I can't do all the things I did in my early days as a believer, but I can remember the heart I had for Jesus in the beginning.

Early in my relationship with God, I'd grab my guitar at 5:00 a.m. and enthusiastically play worship music out of love for Jesus. My neighbors would tell me to shut up, but I didn't care; I wanted everyone to know I loved Jesus. Once, I spent a stupid amount of money (probably a hundred bucks, which was a lot of money to me back then) on custom stickers that read "Jesus is LORD." I put them on the back of my truck. When I drove around, I wanted everyone to know that Jesus is LORD. I wouldn't do that today, because sometimes when I'm driving, I do things that a Christian probably isn't supposed to do while driving. Maybe going a little too fast, maybe not paying attention to the road or other drivers. Imagine people driving behind me thinking, "Some Christian you are." Knowing me, I'd probably say, "Thank you, Jesus, they're persecuting me because I'm standing for you." No, I'm just being a bad driver.

The Bible isn't instructing us to go back to doing the things that we did in the beginning. It's telling us to remember the heart and the passion that drove you to Jesus in the beginning.

The Second "R" is Repent

The simple meaning is to change direction. Turn from where you were heading and go the other way. A deeper definition involves a change of heart and mind. That leads you to turn away from sin and turn toward God, aligning with His will.

The Third "R" is Return to the First Works

Go back and do the things you felt motivated to do in the first place, but do them with that original heart. What drove you to worship God? What drove you to share Christ with people? Maybe you're even doing these things as your profession now, as a pastor or minister, but are you really taking advantage of opportunities with the same heart you used to have?

The truth is sometimes wish I could take the heart I had as a new believer and combine it with the knowledge I have today. I would love God even more now than ever!

On my wedding day, I spoke a promise to her: "I've made the decision that you will become more beautiful to me every day." We should want our heart for the LORD to develop even more intensely than it did in the early days. But it is a choice we must consciously make.

Jesus' View toward the Nicolaitans

Jesus commends the Ephesian church for one more thing:

"But this thou hast, that thou hatest the deeds of the Nicolaitans, which I also hate."

Revelation 2:6

The Nicolaitans were a heretical sect that pretended to be Christlike while dominating the church. They appropriated the roles of priests and told others they could only approach God through them, a power grab designed to rule over everyday people. But their corruption ran deeper. The Nicolaitans also promoted spiritual compromise, suggesting it was permissible for Christians to participate in pagan rituals and sexual immorality without consequence. Thankfully, the church at Ephesus rejected this completely. They refused to tolerate anyone who lorded over God's people and indulged in sinful deeds instead of serving them.

The Promise

> "He that hath an ear, let him hear what the Spirit saith unto the churches; To him that overcometh will I give to eat of the tree of life, which is in the midst of the paradise of God."

Revelation 2:7

This is an important statement from Jesus to the churches. The tree of life means nourishment that sustains you for eternity. If you eat of the tree of life, you live forever. Not just living forever in this nasty world, but living forever in the perfect paradise created by God.

Smyrna: The Persecuted Church

The second letter is to Smyrna, and this one goes quickly because there's no rebuke, only encouragement and warning.

> "And unto the angel of the church in Smyrna write; These things saith the first and the last, which was dead, and is alive;"

Revelation 2:8

Jesus identifies Himself as "the first and the last, which was dead, and is alive." He was there in the beginning, will always be at the end, and He died and rose again.

The Commendation

"I know thy works, and tribulation, and poverty, (but thou art rich) and I know the blasphemy of them which say they are Jews, and are not, but are the synagogue of Satan."

Revelation 2:9

Jesus says, "You guys may be physically poor in this world, but you're actually rich." He knew about their persecution from people claiming to be God's people but wanting nothing to do with God, people who claim to be part of God's family because of their cultural identity but who had walked away from that family.

By the way, there are people, right now, who quote this passage to make the case that Jews are of the synagogue of Satan. But that's not at all what it means. What Jesus is talking about are people who claim to be God's people but want nothing to do with God and completely deny Him. In other words, the context here is they claim to be a part of the family of God because of their cultural or ethnic identity, but they're far from it because they have walked away from His family.

Does it disqualify the Jews from being God's ancestrally chosen people? Absolutely not. Think about this, fathers and mothers: you have a son or daughter who, God forbid, completely separates themselves from you. Imagine they hate you, curse you, and rip you off. They do every terrible thing that you could think of. Are they no longer your son?

Are they no longer your daughter? Of course not! The Jews will always be the children of God. There will always be an ancestral connection to God. Whereas, we as Gentiles were adopted and grafted in.

The Warning and Promise

"Fear none of those things which thou shalt suffer: behold, the devil shall cast some of you into prison, that ye may be tried, and ye shall have tribulation ten days: be thou faithful unto death, and I will give thee a crown of life."

Revelation 2:10

These ten days likely refer to ten different Roman emperors, spanning over two hundred years, starting with Nero and ending with Constantine. It was a time of severe persecution in which Christians were imprisoned and killed at one of the highest rates in world history. If we look at the per capita numbers, it was beyond terrible.

I want to pause here and point something out about the seven letters to the seven churches, because it needs to be emphasized: while these letters do represent specific historical periods, their message is not confined to one era. Each one applies to every church in every age, right up until the rapture.

The reason I can say this with certainty is because of the repeated phrase, "He that hath an ear, let him hear." This phrase is used in every letter that Jesus writes to every church, and the way it is expressed in the Greek language makes it clear that He intended each church to take every message seriously.

These are lessons for all believers in every generation, and they become especially critical for us who are living in these last days.

Jesus says, "Be thou faithful unto death, and I will give thee a crown of life." This statement makes me think about what's happened in recent years. How many Christians have we seen who were faithful unto death, martyred for sake of the Gospel? There are actually a lot of them.

How many Christians have abandoned their faith because of the fear of death? There is a big difference between "being faithful unto death" and abandoning faith because of the fear of death.

For most Christians in the Western world, persecution unto death isn't something they have to deal with. But what if we did? What do we do? We continue to walk in the fear of God. We continue to say, "God, I fear You more than I fear death. I fear You more than I fear anything," and we run to Him, no matter the cost.

I thought about this recently as I watched a video of an active shooting taking place. Local law enforcement officers and federal agents ran toward the shooter while everyone else ran away. I sat there thinking, "These brave men and women knew exactly what they were getting into and didn't retreat." That's what I call faithful unto death. They had no idea if that was going to be their last day alive. They made a choice to protect and serve and ran toward the danger. They embodied those who were willing to be faithful unto death.

As believers we're supposed to say, "No matter what, LORD, we're not going to be fearful, because we trust in You."

When we choose to walk in the fear of God, He says, "You do that and I'm going to reward you."

The Second Death

"He that hath an ear, let him hear what the Spirit saith unto the churches; He that overcometh shall not be hurt of the second death."

Revelation 2:11

I'm so thankful for this promise. The second death refers to eternal separation from God, but faithful believers will never experience it. This is contrasted with the first death, which is physical death. If you don't know the LORD, you're going to experience both the first death and the second death.

Some Christians might not experience the first death if we get raptured before it happens. I can't wait to see people again who have gone before me, my mom, my dad, my grandparents, because the second death never touched them. Because Christ overcame for them!

Pergamos: The Compromising Church

This is where things get very serious.

"And to the angel of the church in Pergamos write; These things saith he which hath the sharp sword with two edges;"

Revelation 2:12

Jesus identifies Himself as "He which hath the sharp sword with two edges." This sword represents the Word of God, the tool that gives us the standard of righteousness and the weapon that will execute judgment on those who reject truth. The sharp sword not only defines the Bible as the rule that sets the standard of righteousness, but it also serves as the tool that allows us to understand the difference between right and wrong. The Word of God is the very thing we stand everything upon.

Notice the other important characteristic Jesus describes: the Word of God is a two-edged sword. One edge serves the beginning of this dual pursuit, where the Body of Christ is being beautifully handled, managed, and cared for. It's like a surgeon performing surgery with precision, going in to deal with something very specific in our hearts. That's what the Word of God does.

The other part of that dichotomy is that the two-edged sword executes a type of judgment that only Jesus can wield. Jesus clarifies that He is the only person who lovingly corrects the Body of Christ through the word He brings, and simultaneously, He alone will judge the world.

Why would Jesus refer to Himself this way unless He's about to deliver a message that requires significant rebuke? That's exactly what we'll see next!

Living Where Satan's Seat Is

"I know thy works, and where thou dwellest, even where Satan's seat is: and thou holdest fast my name, and hast not denied my faith, even in those days wherein Antipas was my faithful martyr, who was slain among you, where Satan dwelleth."

Revelation 2:13

Ancient Pergamos was like what we think of San Francisco or Las Vegas today, a place where Satan held control. Unfortunately, those two cities aren't anomalies. They exist all over the country and throughout the world. Other cities are joining their ranks as the darkness in this world grows, just as the Bible predicted would happen in the last days. If you're a Christian living in a city like this, you know exactly what Jesus means. Satan has a hold on these places and continues to have his way with the people there.

But Jesus commends them: even though they lived where Satan's seat was, they held fast to Jesus and refused to deny their faith, even when facing overwhelming persecution and even death.

Standing up for righteousness can be difficult at times. I remember the COVID pandemic and the day the governor of California declared churches weren't allowed to sing. You could sit within six feet of another person, but you couldn't sing. His crazy thinking was that singing would spread the virus. People had to put on a mask and follow these ridiculous restrictions. I recorded videos telling the governor to pretty much shove off; our church was going to get together and sing anyway. Our church was going to do what we were called to do. We got some pretty heavy pushback. People came against us, including our own city council, who tried to strong-arm me by saying what we were doing was wrong. I made it very clear I wasn't there to ask for their permission. We had a choice: faithfully worship God or obey man's rules.

Taking a stand for righteousness out of obedience to God is one thing. Doing it for attention or the praise of men is something else. Right now, Christians around the world are being murdered for their faithfulness to the LORD. And then there are others, virtue-signaling, who look for opportunities to stand up for the things of God, only to wear persecution like a badge of honor. Don't get me wrong, it's an honor to truly stand up for righteousness, when it's an act of obedience. But lately, something's gone wrong and a mainstream "standing up against evil people" movement popped up. Something changed and a flavor of conservatism emerged and some folks have begun seeking something other than the true God they claimed they were taking a stand for.

First off, Almighty God doesn't need anyone to defend Him. When I say "standing up for righteousness", I'm talking about obeying God's call to worship Him, just like Shadrach, Meshach, and Abednego did in Daniel Chapter 3. But there are people looking for ways to "take a stand," only to draw attention to themselves rather than to God. When the focus shifts from worshiping God because of His virtue, worthiness, and qualities, to simply virtue signaling for a badge of honor, something is terribly wrong.

The Serious Problem: The Doctrine of Balaam

"But I have a few things against thee, because thou hast there them that hold the doctrine of Balaam, who taught Balac to cast a stumbling block before the children of Israel, to eat things sacrificed unto idols, and to commit fornication."

Revelation 2:14

To understand this, we need to go back to another Old Testament story. One day, King Balak summoned a prophet named Balaam and told him to curse Israel (Numbers 22:5–6). The prophet Balaam told Balak that he could only speak what God told him, and that God was going to bless his people, not curse them (Numbers 22:18; Numbers 23:8, 11–12).

But King Balak offered Balaam money, so the prophet devised a workaround to his divine mandate. Balaam's advice went a little something like this: while he couldn't curse Israel directly, Balak could bring in beautiful pagan women to entice the Israelite men. They would fall into fornication and pagan worship. And then, because of their sin, God would bring judgment, and Balak would be able to defeat them (Numbers 25:1–3; Numbers 31:16; Revelation 2:14).

And that's exactly what happened. We now call this corrupt approach the doctrine of Balaam: twisting your knowledge of God's Word to manipulate outcomes for your own benefit, which ultimately destroys God's people.

The prophet Balaam led God's people into destruction for his own personal gain. And for what? To line his pockets a little? Perhaps he wanted to gain some notoriety or Balak's approval. But by manipulating the law and abusing his position as one of God's prophets, he actually destroyed the very people he was called to serve.

Today's Applications

This happens a lot, even in churches today. Pastors intentionally make a "list of things" they will never preach about because they fear people will get mad, stop attending church, or withhold their giving. They won't address the horror of abortion, they refuse to engage with political issues, and many even sanitize their messages, avoiding certain terms or pronouns like "he" or "she," in order to appear neutral on controversial issues. But here's the problem: when they do this at the expense of speaking the truth, they're lining their pockets while leading people to spiritual death. Some pastors go even further, twisting Scripture to get people to accept worldly philosophy. They create outcomes favorable to themselves so they can gain the notoriety they crave.

There are pastors in some churches who sound more like secular humanists, instructing people to accept things that God rejects. I've even heard them talk about "how to be more graceful than God." I can drive down the street today and see pride flags hanging outside some churches. Sadly, I've seen so-called Christian leaders who, for their own benefit will lie about everything under the sun.

The Doctrine of the Nicolaitans

"So hast thou also them that hold the doctrine of the Nicolaitans, which thing I hate."

Revelation 2:15

Again, Jesus mentions "the doctrine of the Nicolaitans, which thing I hate." We covered this with the Ephesian church, but it bears repeating: these are people who lord over God's people instead of serving them, creating a hierarchy that puts themselves between people and God.

The Ultimatum

"Repent; or else I will come unto thee quickly, and will fight against them with the sword of my mouth."

Revelation 2:16

The same Word of God that these false teachers twist for their own gain will ultimately be the Word that destroys them. Later in Revelation, there's a vivid description of God speaking a single word and annihilating all his enemies.

Think about the weight of that exhortation. As a pastor, I'm terrified of the consequences of misleading God's people. It's an honor and a precious thing to shepherd God's people, and I never take it lightly.

Pastors should instead dedicate ourselves to teaching God's Word in its pure form, without changing the Bible. It's the most effective tool we have. That's why we should teach the Word of God exactly as it was intended.

The apostle Paul wrote in 2 Timothy 2:15 about "rightly dividing the word of truth." This means we must accurately interpret and apply the Bible in its proper context, never distorting or misrepresenting God's Word for personal gain or to win others' approval. God assesses how we handle His Word, so we must study it diligently to grow in our faith and help others grow in theirs. Paul reminds us that when we are diligent in this calling, we won't need to be ashamed, because we will have been faithful with the sacred stewardship God has entrusted to us. And God has make it very clear: judgment awaits people who play around with His Word.

The Promise for Overcomers

"He that hath an ear, let him hear what the Spirit saith unto the churches; To him that overcometh will I give to eat of the hidden manna;"

Revelation 2:17

People who compromise almost always do it for three things: money, power, and notoriety. However, the money they get is blood money that will burn, the notoriety they gain becomes infamy, and the power they acquire becomes their weakness. Jesus promises something far better for those who overcome. Hidden manna means God will provide for you in ways you can't even imagine. You won't know where it's coming from, but God will meet your needs.

I've lost track of how many times the church I pastor has faced situations we knew would hurt us financially. We either had to go with what the world would do, or we had to stick with what God has taught us and trust that He would provide. Many times it looked like we were going to lose everything, Nevertheless, we chose to do what God told us to do. Not only did He provide for us, He provided in ways that made us say, "Where in the world did that come from? How did that even happen?" Because God gave us hidden manna.

> "and will give him a white stone, and in the stone a new name written, which no man knoweth saving he that receiveth it."
>
> **Revelation 2:17**

The white stone with a new name means God will recognize you as the individual He made you to be. It's not some automated, mass-produced, impersonal, AI-generated label. God is telling you that He'll not only give you food prepared specifically for you to eat, He is giving you a new, uniquely personal name that only you and He will know. It's a special, intimate thing between you and God.

The Spiritual Battle of Our Time

In these last days, the enemy will do everything he can to get you to accept what is fake. We're being told we can find fulfillment in materialism, relationships with computers, and the ultimate VR world constructed by man. As the world grows accustomed to the AI age, more people are accepting fictitious versions of relationships and intimacy. Social media feeds follow algorithms designed to convince you that something has been made just for you, when in reality, there's nothing real about it. The Bible says it's all garbage.

Instead, God says, "Forget all that. I've got something better. I'm going to nourish your soul in ways you've never been nourished, and I'm going to give you something real, intimate, and powerful."

Think of the most incredible thing you've ever experienced on this earth. That will be nothing compared to heaven. God has what's real, and He wants to give it to you.

Looking at the first three churches in Revelation chapter two (Ephesus, Smyrna, and Pergamos), there's a clear pattern that continues throughout the seven letters. Truth without love becomes cold orthodoxy. Love without truth becomes dangerous compromise. Both are deadly. Only what God offers is truly real.

In the next chapter, we'll look at what Jesus had to say to the churches of Thyatira, Sardis, Philadelphia, and Laodicea. Don't compromise and become like the world. Be faithful and strengthen what remains. And do not be lukewarm.

3
A Church in Crisis

The church today faces a crisis. We're living in the last days, and as we draw closer to the end, the stakes are getting higher. The warnings that keep coming are designed to give us direction and insight, both for the life we're living now and the life that's to come.

Thyatira: The Church That Tolerated Jezebel

Now we come to one of the most serious letters Jesus delivered.

> "And unto the angel of the church in Thyatira write; These things saith the Son of God, who hath his eyes like unto a flame of fire, and his feet are like fine brass;"

Revelation 2:18

Why would Jesus refer to Himself this way unless He's about to deliver a message that requires serious rebuke? His eyes like flames of fire mean His vision is piercing, He sees everything clearly, down to the heart's hidden corners. His feet like fine brass speak of the power to execute judgment and provide redemption. This isn't a gentle greeting; it's a warning that what follows will be weighty and direct.

When we talk about brass, understand that it was one of the strongest and most reliable metals of that time. It couldn't have been polluted with impurities, brass was highly refined and pure.

Let's look at another example of why the Old Testament is so important for understanding this. When we read about the construction of the tabernacle in The Book of Exodus, we see that brass consistently symbolized judgment. The altar of burnt offering was made of brass and overlaid with brass because it was where sin was judged through sacrifice (Exodus 27:1–2). The laver where the priests washed before ministering was also made of brass (Exodus 30:18), a constant reminder that cleansing was required in the presence of a holy God. Brass stood as the metal of judgment against sin.

This symbolism appears again in the wilderness, when the people of Israel sinned and were plagued by fiery serpents. God instructed Moses to lift up a brass serpent on a pole, and those who looked upon it were healed (Numbers 21:9). That act foreshadowed Christ being lifted up on the cross (John 3:14–15), where judgment and redemption converged.

When Revelation describes Christ with feet like fine brass, it carries all this weight. On one hand, it points to His role as Judge. He sees justly and has the power to execute judgment. On the other hand, it points to redemption, because judgment and mercy meet in Him. The picture deepens when we recall the prophecy of Genesis 3:15, where Satan bruised the heel of Christ. Now in Revelation, that same heel is described as refined brass: purified, strong, and unbreakable. The heel once bruised now becomes the instrument of judgment against Satan and, at the same time, the assurance of redemption for those who trust in Him.

Notice Jesus' commends the church in Thyatira:

"I know thy works, and charity, and service, and faith, and thy patience, and thy works; and the last to be more than the first."

Revelation 2:19

This sounds like He's describing a pretty healthy church! They had love, service, faith, and patience, and their recent works were even better than their first ones. They didn't leave people behind. Instead, they went out of their way to find the suffering, the poor, and the weak to show them God's love.

No other organization in history has served humanity better than some churches have. They've fought important fights, introduced people to Jesus, and done incredible works of service.

But then comes the devastating rebuke.

The Serious Problem

"Notwithstanding I have a few things against thee, because thou sufferest that woman Jezebel, which calleth herself a prophetess, to teach and to seduce my servants to commit fornication, and to eat things sacrificed unto idols."

Revelation 2:20

We need to go back to the Old Testament to understand

who Jezebel was. She was married to King Ahab of Israel. She was a demonic woman, very likely the most wicked woman in the Bible. What made her extraordinarily evil wasn't just her actions, it was the sheer depths of depravity she reached.

Jezebel is perhaps most infamous for introducing and aggressively promoting the worship of the false god, Baal, in Israel. She and her prophets gave themselves over to idolatry and sexual immorality as part of this evil worship, filling the land with idols and statues. But she didn't stop there. She actively persecuted the prophets of the LORD, killing most of them in a deliberate attempt to eliminate any opposition to Baal.

Jezebel's wickedness is also made clear in the story of Naboth's vineyard (1 Kings 21). When Naboth refused to sell his inheritance to King Ahab, Jezebel devised a plan to have him falsely accused and executed, allowing the land to be seized. This act revealed just how far she would go to exploit and destroy the innocent for her own gain.

We also see Jezebel's hand in the infamous showdown on Mount Carmel (1 Kings 18), when Elijah confronted the prophets of Baal. After God's undeniable victory, Jezebel refused to repent. Instead, she doubled down on her wickedness by threatening to kill Elijah.

This is evidence of Jezebel's relentless rebellion against the LORD, deep-seated hatred of truth, and willingness to destroy anyone who dared stand in the way of her false worship.

Jezebel's Spirit in Today's World

In today's world, we see the metaphorical spirit of Jezebel

everywhere. Countless things pull us away from the true living God, certain TV shows and streaming platforms, social media, music, and entertainment. Most are designed to develop what I call a "fornication mindset," an adulterous attitude that pushes people away from a committed relationship with God.

I've often seen people browse Instagram, look at news sites, and do all kinds of things while listening to a Bible study. Make no mistake, this is designed to shift their focus from the LORD to the things of the world. When we let these distractions take precedence over our relationship with God, it becomes a serious problem.

The church of Thyatira tolerated Jezebel as she introduced foreign and false gods. They looked the other way and let her do these things. What makes this even more serious is that God, in His mercy, gave her the opportunity to repent, yet she refused.

> "And I gave her space to repent of her fornication, and she repented not."
>
> **Revelation 2:21**

This verse reveals both the patience of the LORD in giving time for repentance and the hardness of Jezebel's heart in rejecting it. The judgment that follows isn't because God was unwilling to forgive, but because she stubbornly chose to remain in rebellion. I don't know exactly what it looked like for God to give her space to repent. Was there a moment when God got the attention of this false prophetess?

Did the church of Thyatira get caught up in something that nearly wrecked them, and did they recognize the LORD was sending them a warning? We don't know for certain, but the Bible tells us Jezebel had that opportunity to repent and turn from her ways, and she didn't take it.

The Ultimate "Mess Around and Find Out"

"Behold, I will cast her into a bed, and them that commit adultery with her into great tribulation, except they repent of their deeds. And I will kill her children with death."

Revelation 2:22

This is God saying, "You've made your bed, now lie in it. I'll let you keep the destructive system you've created and live with the consequences."

Think about smart parents who create consequences their children can understand to protect them from consequences they can't understand. My father did this. He'd discipline me in a way I could understand, like a spanking when I ran into the street. The real consequence of that action could have been death, but as a child, I couldn't grasp that reality. I lacked the life experience. So my father wisely created a consequence I could understand to shield me from the one I couldn't.

When we were little, we'd kick the ball around in the front yard, and my dad would always say, "When the ball leaves the yard, let me get it." Every time the ball rolled into the street, we'd wait for him to turn off the lawnmower and get it. Then there were times we got impatient and ignored his warning.

I remember as a little guy, standing in between my dad's cherry-red '65 Mustang and my mom's big Chrysler station wagon. I'd spot the ball through the gap in the cars and bolt into the street to grab it. Every time I did, my dad would spank me. I hated the sting in the moment, but that's how I learned not to run into harm's way.

At three years old, my only thought was, "If I run into the street, Dad's going to spank me." But years later, when I became a police chaplain and consoled families who'd lost a child struck by a car, I finally understood what my father had known all along. The real consequence was far worse than any spanking. In his wisdom and love, my dad created a consequence I could understand in order to protect me from the one I couldn't.

But here, God is saying something really serious: "I'm going to let them experience the real consequences of their actions." That's the ultimate definition of messing around and finding out.

But notice what God has to say to the faithful ones:

> "But unto you I say, and unto the rest in Thyatira, as many as have not this doctrine, and which have not known the depths of Satan, as they speak, I will put upon you none other burden. But that which ye have already hold fast till I come."

Revelation 2:24

For those who haven't gotten caught up in this spiritual adultery, God says, "Hold fast till I come. Don't worship false gods. Don't let yourself slip into an adulterous relationship where you're no longer seeking the true God."

With that exhortation also comes a beautiful, powerful promise from God.

> "And he that overcometh, and keepeth my works unto the end, to him will I give power over the nations; and he shall rule them with a rod of iron; as the vessels of a potter shall they be broken to shivers, even as I also received of my Father. And I will give him the morning star."

Revelation 2:26-27

The morning star means hope. When they saw the morning star, it meant a new dawn was coming. Jesus is saying here, "I'm going to give you Me." What can be better than that?

Sardis: The Church with a Great Name but No Life

We kick off Revelation Chapter 3 with the next letter, to Sardis, and this one hits very close to home for many of us today.

> "And unto the angel of the church in Sardis write; These things saith he that hath the seven Spirits of God, and the seven stars; I know thy works, that thou hast a name that thou livest, and art dead."

Revelation 3:1

That's a heavy statement. This was a church whose name meant life itself, and yet nothing about them actually represented life.

Let me get personal for a moment. There was a time when the name Calvary Chapel carried weight everywhere. You could tell someone, "I go to Calvary Chapel," and their face would light up. They'd share stories about Chuck Smith, about Jesus hippies meeting in a tent, about all the incredible things

God was doing.

I traveled to Israel when I was 17 years old, and went through a security checkpoint at Ben-Gurion Airport. Now, when I speak English, you can't detect any foreign accent. But when I speak Arabic, it's clear I was born and raised in Egypt. I was overheard speaking Arabic, which turned out to be a massive mistake. I got pulled aside for interrogation. An Israeli security officer started firing tough questions at me, machine-gun style: "Why are you here? What church are you with?" His face completely changed the moment I replied, "Calvary Chapel." His expression shifted from intimidating interrogation to a massive smile. He started telling me how Chuck Smith had bought ambulances for Israel and how Calvary Chapel had built such a good reputation there. He told me, "When you're in Jerusalem and you see all those ambulances going through the streets, you can thank your pastor, because he bought those for us."

I learned that Chuck had received money from a billionaire who wanted to donate to Calvary Chapel. Chuck told him, "Don't give to Calvary Chapel. Give that money to Israel and God will bless you." The billionaire gave the money to Calvary Chapel anyway, and Chuck used it to purchase dozens of ambulances for Israel. When Chuck died in 2013, Israel's Knesset ordered its flag flown at half-staff for several days.

Back then, you could mention Calvary Chapel's name to a bank, and they'd give you a loan without hesitation because they knew the churches paid their bills. The Calvary Chapel name carried that much weight.

I hate to say it, but that's not the case today. The Calvary

Chapel name has been dragged through the mud on multiple fronts, leading to a slow decline. What was once a vibrant, trusted name has steadily lost its strength.

Does that mean we're done? No. God has a way of reviving things when we let Him. But when I see a letter like this written to Sardis, I pay special attention.

> "Be watchful, and strengthen the things which remain, that are ready to die; for I have not found thy works perfect before God."
>
> **Revelation 3:2**

Being watchful also means staying sober-minded while you observe. Two people can examine the same information and reach completely different conclusions.

Let me give you an example. Our air conditioner broke down once. We tried to fix it, starting with the basics. We pulled the fuses and tried to reset the unit, but nothing worked. We asked a handy friend to take a look and he quickly realized it was beyond his ability to diagnose or repair. So I called an experienced HVAC guy from our church. He gets on the phone, asks a few questions, and immediately says, "Yeah, it's this. Here's the problem." He knew exactly how to fix it, and boom, it was done! Two different people looking at the same situation but coming to completely different conclusions.

It's not enough to simply watch, you need to be watching with intention, while you're sober-minded.

When God says to strengthen what remains, He's telling you to take whatever little health you have left and strengthen it by doing what's right.

My Personal Journey

Allow me to share another personal story. When I first started our church, I weighed over 700 pounds and was told I wouldn't live to see 30. I decided to get healthy, but I quickly learned something: when you're unhealthy, you don't enjoy doing healthy things. Healthy activities contradict everything that got you unhealthy in the first place. So I started simple, standing up and sitting down five or six times. I hated every minute of it. It was painful. But Greg, the guy helping me who'd served on the Olympic board for physiology, gave it to me straight: "You have two choices. Give up, and I'll be there when they take you away in a hearse, or fight and get healthy."

Exercising was excruciating. I'd walk forty feet to a weight bench, and by the time I got there, I was already exhausted and in pain. I remember the anxiety building up a day or two before each session. Once it got so bad that Greg just sat there and started crying. I knew exactly why. I knew he was thinking, "James is circling the drain. He's going to die."

But by God's grace, I kept at it. I lost about 350 pounds, and today, I get anxious if I don't get to do my daily 19-mile bike ride. So what changed? At my heaviest, I was so sick I was literally moments from death, and exercise was the last thing I wanted to do. But once I turned a corner and started getting healthy, I wanted to keep going. Unhealthy habits now contradicted my healthy mindset and actions.

Spiritually, it works the same way. People come to me and say, "I hate reading the Bible." If you're struggling with the Bible, understand that you're spiritually sick. But if you commit to getting spiritually healthy by strengthening what remains, you'll soon look forward to reading the Bible and feel anxious when you can't.

It's a telltale symptom of spiritual sickness when reading the Bible and spending time with God becomes a burden. Something is seriously wrong, but nurse yourself back to health, strengthen what remains, and God will help you.

The Warning About Christ's Coming

> "Remember therefore how thou hast received and heard, and hold fast, and repent. If therefore thou shalt not watch, I will come on thee as a thief, and thou shalt not know what hour I will come upon thee."

Revelation 3:3

If you take the Bible literally and hold fast, awaiting Christ's return, you won't be surprised when He comes. You'll be like, "It's about time!" But if you're not watching, His coming will catch you completely off guard. Christians should develop spiritual awareness and learn to react instinctively to what's happening around them. If you're not watching what's taking place spiritually, you're going to get blindsided and caught unaware when Jesus returns like a thief in the night. Someone once said, and it still holds true: "Live like Jesus died yesterday, rose today, and is returning tomorrow."

> "Thou hast a few names even in Sardis which have not defiled their garments; and they shall walk with me in white: for they are worthy."

Revelation 3:4

Jesus commends the few true believers in the church

at Sardis for maintaining their spiritual purity despite the community's widespread spiritual decline. God declares that even when everyone rejects Him, those who stand for Him, are counted as worthy.

Many of you stood against what the world demanded when the COVID nonsense started happening. You attended a church that remained open, and you grew stronger spiritually. Since then, our lives have changed radically, never to be the same again. Why? Because God is faithful. I had people in their 80s coming to our church who told me, "I'd rather die free than live trapped in a cage."

When a remnant like that takes a stand for righteousness, God rewards them immensely.

Philadelphia: The Church with an Open Door

In Revelation 3:7-13, we get to the letter to Philadelphia, and it brings a ton of hope because there's no rebuke, only encouragement and promise. Long before the American city with the same name was founded, Philadelphia was a city in Lydia, which is now modern-day Turkey. The name means "brotherly love." This city was the youngest of the seven cities, founded as an outreach center for Hellenism to teach people Greek language and culture.

Jesus identifies Himself as "He that is holy, He that is true, He that hath the key of David, He that openeth and no man shutteth; and shutteth, and no man openeth."

Holy means set aside, dedicated, and consecrated to God. When I think of holiness, I think of intention and purpose. Jesus was set aside for a very specific purpose: to save the world. That's exactly what He came to do, and what He accomplished.

When Jesus speaks of having the key of David, He's declaring His authority over everything associated with His kingly rule. One day, He'll be revealed as King of Kings and LORD of Lords (Revelation 19:16).

This authority traces back to King David, who looked from his palace one day and saw the tent where the ark of the covenant was kept. He said, "How can I live in a house of cedar while the ark of God remains in a tent?" He then resolved to build a house for the LORD (2 Samuel 7:2). At first, the prophet Nathan encouraged King David, but later the LORD corrected Nathan, making it clear that David wouldn't build the temple because he had shed too much blood (2 Samuel 7:5–6; 1 Chronicles 22:8).

Instead, God allowed David to gather the materials while his son Solomon oversaw the temple's construction (1 Kings 5–6).

But the covenant made with David through Nathan went far beyond the temple. God promised David that a King from his lineage would establish a throne and kingdom that would endure forever (2 Samuel 7:12–16; Psalm 89:3–4, 34–37). This is the Davidic covenant, and Jesus Christ is its ultimate fulfillment. Both genealogies in the Gospels confirm His right to the throne.

Matthew Chapter 1 traces the royal line through Solomon, showing Jesus' legal right to rule, but that line also carried the curse of Jeconiah (Jeremiah 22:30). Luke's genealogy traces through Nathan, another son of David, showing a bloodline free from that curse.

It's important to understand that the genealogy listed in Matthew is tied to Joseph, Jesus' legal father. Because Jesus was conceived by the Holy Spirit, He had no blood connection to that cursed line. The true bloodline came through Mary, His mother, which is recorded in Luke's account. Her lineage traces back to David through Nathan, preserving the promise without the curse. In this way, both genealogies validate that Jesus is the only One who could fulfill the covenant promises to David and rightly be the Messiah.

This covenant carries consequences that reach far beyond David's lifetime. It points directly to the Messiah who will one day rule the entire world in perpetuity, when He takes back the title deed of the earth as described in Revelation 5. It also declares His present authority, because He alone is the One "that is holy, He that is true, He that hath the key of David, He that openeth and no man shutteth, and shutteth and no man openeth" (Revelation 3:7).

This is also why Israel matters so much. God's promise to Israel has not been broken. If His covenant with Israel were to fail, then our salvation itself would collapse, because our salvation rests on the everlasting rule of the descendant of David. You cannot separate the two. The certainty of our salvation is bound up in God's faithfulness to Israel, and His promises to Israel guarantee the promises we cling to today.

The Open Door Promise

"I know thy works: behold, I have set before thee an open door, and no man can shut it: for thou hast little strength, and hast kept my word, and hast not denied my name."

Revelation 3:8

This is Jesus saying, "I know you have very limited resources. You're weak. You've been through a lot. But you haven't turned your back on the truth. I'm the one who put you in this position. I opened this door for you to walk through, and I promise you, no one is shutting it."

Many believers, including myself, have found ourselves in places where it feels like there's no energy left, weak and totally drained on every level. But when we look back, we can see that God brought us through the times we didn't think we could survive. Even in our weakness, the LORD opened doors that nobody could shut.

In 2020, when COVID hit, God told me I would have to go in one direction while my colleagues went in another. It cost me nearly every friend and close relationship I had.

My calendar went from 200 to 300 speaking engagements a year to crickets. I went from being the guy pastors wanted to be around to suddenly being the guy they secretly reached out to, asking me not to tell anyone they'd called.

No one wanted the "controversial guy." People kicked me out of groups and told me to leave. The reputation I'd worked years to build was completely washed away.

But then, as only He can do, God began opening doors I'd never even imagined possible. Now I can't leave my state without someone recognizing me.

I'll tell you a funny story. I was at a Texas airport going

through TSA with my mobility scooter when one particular TSA employee started giving me a really hard time. He was trying to force me through a line my scooter wouldn't fit through. Suddenly, a federal Homeland Security agent with his bomb-sniffing dog walked up and told the TSA employee, "Let him through right over there. He's fine. I personally vouch for him."

As I passed through, relieved and curious about what had just happened, the agent leaned over and whispered in my ear, "God bless you, Pastor James. Love your ministry!" God has a way of providing exactly what you need when you do things His way.

Dealing With False Teachers

"Behold, I will make them of the synagogue of Satan, which say they are Jews, and are not, but do lie. Behold, I will make them to come and worship before thy feet, and to know that I have loved thee."

Revelation 3:9

This verse isn't talking about Jews no longer being God's chosen people, as some claim. That's hogwash and a satanic lie. Remember, God made a promise to Abraham. In the Book of Jeremiah, God says, "Look up. Do you see the sun, stars, moon? As long as those ordinances exist, so will the mercy I show my people Israel." God calls Israel the apple of His eye. We got our life, our salvation, everything through a Jew.

Jesus is specifically addressing a group who claim to follow God but deny the true, living God. He promises the faithful believers in Philadelphia that these pretenders will one day bow down and acknowledge the church's legitimacy, and recognize that God truly loves His people.

The Promise of Rapture

"Because thou hast kept the word of my patience, I also will keep thee from the hour of temptation, which shall come upon all the world, to try them that dwell upon the earth."

Revelation 3:10

This is Jesus promising to keep us from the tribulation. The time of tribulation will be God's judgment on the world for their hatred against Him, persecuting His chosen people (the Jews), and opposing believers. It's also when He'll draw the Jewish people back to Himself.

"Behold, I come quickly: hold that fast which thou hast, that no man take thy crown."

Revelation 3:11

When you feel like you have nothing left, remember: you have a Father who loves you, a Messiah who saved you, and a Holy Spirit who lives inside you. God calls us to cling to that truth. It's all we need to do. No one can take your crown if you hold on to the LORD.

Jesus could return for His church at any moment. What if He came before you finished reading this book? The moment could arrive without warning. Biblically, nothing else needs to happen before Christ comes for His church. Only God knows when. As believers, we need only to faithfully follow Jesus and wait for His return.

The Pillar Promise

"Him that overcometh will I make a pillar in the temple of my God, and he shall go no more out: and I will write upon him the name of my God, and the name of the city of my God, which is New Jerusalem, which cometh down out of heaven from my God: and I will write upon him my new name."

Revelation 3:12

God promises to make you a pillar in His temple. Pillars represent strength, stability, and something unshakable, part of a building's permanent foundation. Though you're weak now, you'll be eternally strong when you overcome by holding fast. Ancient Philadelphia faced constant earthquakes, and unstable buildings would crumble under the pressure.

So when God says you'll be a pillar in New Jerusalem, He's painting an incredible picture: something permanent, strong, and stable with no uncertainty. And the new name Jesus promises to write on you won't be some generic number from a massive spreadsheet. Your identity will be rooted in something intimate, a name chosen just for you and nobody else.

Laodicea: The Church God Spit Out

Finally, we reach what is one of the most incorrectly taught passages in all of Revelation. This is God's final warning to the church, and it speaks more directly to the American church today than at any other time in history.

"And unto the angel of the church of the Laodiceans write; These things saith the Amen, the faithful and true witness, the beginning of the creation of God;"

Revelation 3:14

Jesus identifies Himself as "the Amen, the faithful and true witness, the beginning of the creation of God." Amen means "so be it." Jesus speaks as One whose words are absolute and unchanging. When He declares something, it's as good as done. There's no possibility it won't happen.

Jesus is the faithful and true witness, which means He never misrepresents truth, He's consistent with everyone. He's the beginning of God's creation. He was present when everything was spoken into existence. His word carries such power that He spoke all of creation into being.

> "I know thy works, that thou art neither cold nor hot: I would thou wert cold or hot. So then because thou art lukewarm, and neither cold nor hot, I will spue thee out of my mouth."

Revelation 3:15-16

And here's where everyone gets it wrong.

The common teaching is that "cold" means hating God, "hot" means loving God, and "lukewarm" means being on the fence. That teaching is completely wrong. Nothing could be further from the truth.

God would never want you to hate Him. The Bible says He takes no pleasure in the death of the wicked. He desires everyone to come to repentance. There's no scenario where God earnestly wishes you would become His enemy.

Both hot and cold are good things. They're refreshing

extremes. Cold refreshes you on a hot day, and hot refreshes you on a cold day. The metaphor here is about drinking something. Think about it, on a cold winter day, nothing beats a hot beverage. I was in Russia once when it was -20°F outside, thinking, "I'd give anything for a hot cup of coffee right now." And on a scorching day, there's nothing like a tall glass of ice-cold water. Both extremes refresh you in their own way.

But lukewarm? That's when you expect something refreshing and get tepid liquid the same temperature as your mouth. It's useless, and you just want to spit it out.

By the way, it's worth noting that the Greek word translated "cold" here is ψυχρός (psuchrós). This word appears only one other time in the New Testament, when Jesus said, "And whosoever shall give to drink unto one of these little ones a cup of cold (ψυχροῦ) water only in the name of a disciple, verily I say unto you, he shall in no wise lose his reward" (Matthew 10:42).

This connection confirms that "cold" in Revelation 3 doesn't represent spiritual deadness, but rather something refreshing and good in its own right.

Personality and Spiritual Temperature

Hot and cold reflect your personality in serving God. I'm hot, meaning, I'm loud, energetic, and passionate. People complain that my voice is too loud, but that's who I am. That's how God made me, and I'm not going to let it bother me.

Chuck Smith was cold. We wasn't cold-hearted, but quiet, measured, and mild-mannered. I regularly listen to Chuck Smith, but I put him on 2x speed because he talks so slowly.

But he was brilliantly cold.

Billy Graham was hot. Pastor Chuck was cold. My wife is as cold as they come, very reserved. We all have different personalities, and God wants us to be refreshing extremes according to who He made us to be.

If you're cold, be refreshingly cold for God. If you're hot, be refreshingly hot for God. But don't be lukewarm, don't refuse to live the way God called you to live.

I don't think there are genuine Christians who are lukewarm. If you're lukewarm, you've likely never been regenerated by the Spirit of God. You're not governed by the same Spirit that governs those who are hot or cold.

Self-Deception

"Because thou sayest, I am rich, and increased with goods, and have need of nothing; and knowest not that thou art wretched, and miserable, and poor, and blind, and naked."

Revelation 3:17

The church in Laodicea was using the world's standards to measure their success instead of God's standards. How many churches today measure success by buildings, budgets, and attendance instead of what God says matters?

How many times have you seen pastors getting excited about new buildings, spending more time focused on the structure than on the One who's building it? When we spend more time trying to understand Google Analytics than the analytics of the Holy Spirit, we've got a serious problem.

The Solution: Pursue God's Gold

"I counsel thee to buy of me gold tried in the fire, that thou mayest be rich; and white raiment, that thou mayest be clothed, and that the shame of thy nakedness do not appear; and anoint thine eyes with eyesalve, that thou mayest see."

Revelation 3:18

Stop buying fool's gold from the world. Go find God's gold and let the Word of God be your value system. Don't let the world's values become your values. When you place a premium on what God values, you'll always find the greater gain.

I remember my mom telling me something valuable when I got a job offer that could have made me substantial money. She said, "James, don't ever let the world tell you what to place your time and energy on. What it gives you in exchange will never be as valuable as what you give the LORD. Look at everything God has provided for your father and me. We did it by trusting in God and knowing He would provide."

God honors you every time you place value on His values and reject the world's value system.

"As many as I love, I rebuke and chasten: be zealous therefore, and repent."

Revelation 3:19

Notice it's not just "repent", it's "be zealous and repent." Go back to being extreme. Get out there and live that extreme life God called you to live according to your personality.

My YouTube ministry is a direct result of making that decision in a new area of my life. When COVID went down, I was at a crossroads. I could do what everyone else was doing and play it safe, or I could walk with great zeal. That's what I've been doing, and I've loved every minute of it.

> "Behold, I stand at the door, and knock: if any man hear my voice, and open the door, I will come in to him, and will sup with him, and he with me."

Revelation 3:20

God is knocking on the door of every heart. He doesn't promise to terrorize you, He promises to sit down and dine with you, to commune with you intimately. The closer you draw to Christ, the more power you gain to overcome what seems impossible.

Even when everything feels broken beyond repair, insurmountable and overwhelming, God says you don't need to have all the answers. The only thing He asks is that you trust Him. Open the door, let Him in, and He'll help you overcome.

The Ultimate Promise

> "To him that overcometh will I grant to sit with me in my throne, even as I also overcame, and am set down with my Father in his throne."

Revelation 3:21

You receive the reward because Christ overcame, not because of anything you did. You get to be the recipient of that benefit. There's an inheritance waiting for you, and it was fully His work, not yours!

The Crisis and the Hope

We've examined four churches that reveal the same crises confronting today's church.

Thyatira warns us against tolerating false teaching and spiritual adultery. We must not compromise with the world's system.

Sardis warns us against having a reputation for being spiritually alive while, actually being spiritually dead. We must stay watchful and strengthen what remains.

Philadelphia shows us the faithful church that holds fast to God's Word despite having little strength. God opens doors that no one can shut.

Laodicea warns us against becoming lukewarm, neither hot nor cold, and measuring success by worldly standards instead of God's. It shows us how destructive apathy becomes when it settles in, robbing us of everything God has for us.

When we look at the church today, we see all these problems playing out. But the church is in crisis, not hopeless. God still has His faithful remnant. He still opens doors that no one can shut. He still rewards those who overcome.

The Final Warning and Promise

Make no mistake, we're living in the final hour. This isn't just a figure of speech, it's a period of time defined by God Himself. Remember, His timing isn't the same as ours (2 Peter 3:8), which is why it's so important to recognize how little time we actually have. The church is officially on notice, and we must pay close attention to these warnings. If we don't, we're in serious trouble.

But for those who overcome, the promises are spectacular: power over the nations with Christ, becoming pillars in God's temple, receiving a new name written by God Himself, sitting with Christ on His throne, eating from the tree of life, and receiving the Morning Star, Christ Himself.

The church may be in crisis, but God is faithful. Christ could come at any moment for His church. Make sure you're found faithful when He appears.

Be hot or cold, never lukewarm. Hold fast to truth. Don't leave your first love. Be willing to suffer for His name. Refuse to compromise.

The One who promises these things is faithful and true. He has never failed to keep a promise. He's not going to start now.

What Happens After the Rapture

Before we dive into Revelation Chapter 4, I want to take you back to Revelation 1:19, because this verse is absolutely crucial to understanding the entire book of Revelation. This is literally the key to understanding how this prophetic book is structured. When Jesus appears to John, He gives him very specific instructions.

> "Write the things which thou hast seen, and the things which are, and the things which shall be hereafter."

Revelation 1:19

If you understand this verse, you'll understand that the book of Revelation is broken up into three distinct sections:

1. The things John had seen.
2. The things that currently are.
3. The things that will come hereafter.

This isn't just a casual observation; it's the divine outline God gave us for interpreting this entire prophetic book.

Revelation chapter one represents the things John had

seen. Revelation Chapters 2 and 3 represent the things which are: the Church Age we're currently living in. And Chapter 4 marks the beginning of something we haven't yet witnessed: the things that will come.

This distinction is absolutely crucial. If you don't understand how God organized this book, you'll struggle to interpret Revelation as a whole. So many aspects of this prophecy simply can't be understood without recognizing the divine structure God has laid out for us.

After This: A Critical Transition

It's no coincidence that Chapter 4 opens with "after this." Some Bible translations interpret it "after these things." In Greek, the phrase is μετὰ ταῦτα (meta tauta). This is significant because it connects directly back to Revelation 1:19.

When John says "after these things," he's referring to the sequence given earlier: after the things John had seen (Chapter 1) and after the things which are (Chapters 2–3, the Church Age we're currently in). In other words, meta tauta signals that at this point in the vision, the church has been raptured, and now John is being shown what follows.

We're currently living in the Church Age, which aligns perfectly with the seven letters written to the seven churches. The principles laid out in these letters remarkably apply to what we see in churches today. The seven churches represent specific historical periods, but they also represent characteristics that exist in every church right now.

So what happens between the Church Age described in Revelation Chapter 2–3 and what we see in Chapter 4? Let's look at verse one:

> "After this I looked, and, behold, a door was opened in heaven: and the first voice which I heard was as it were of a trumpet talking with me; which said, Come up hither, and I will shew thee things which must be hereafter."

Revelation 4:1

Notice that phrase again: "things which must be hereafter" (the same phrase from Revelation 1:19). There's the sound of a trumpet, and then John is taken up. I believe what we're witnessing in Revelation 4:1, is a depiction of the rapture. John is seeing it enacted, and it's very clear what's happening.

Addressing the Rapture Biblically

I need to pause here and address the subject of the rapture, because there's an incredible amount of opposition and even hatred toward this biblical doctrine. Frankly, it's insane. I believe there's satanic opposition at work whenever we deal with the subject of the rapture or anything related to end-times matters.

I see this opposition constantly. People throw out various arguments: "The word 'rapture' isn't even in the Bible," they say. "It's just a fairy tale." At this point, I often don't even respond to people who make such statements, because when they say things like that, they're actively demonstrating their ignorance of biblical languages. They clearly don't understand how our modern manuscripts work or where these terms originated.

It's true, the English word "rapture" isn't in any Bible

translation. But that doesn't mean the concept isn't biblical. In 1 Thessalonians 4:17, Paul uses the Greek verb ἁρπάζω (harpazō), which means "to seize, snatch away, or carry off by force." When Jerome translated the Greek New Testament into Latin (the Vulgate), he used the word rapiemur (from rapturo, the future passive of rapio, meaning "to seize" or "to carry away"). From that Latin word we get our English term "rapture."

The issue, then, isn't whether the English word "rapture" appears in the Bible, it doesn't. The issue is whether the Bible describes the event itself, and it absolutely does. Remember, the Bible was originally written in three languages: Hebrew, Aramaic, and Greek. It was translated into other languages later, including Latin. One of those Latin manuscripts, the Vulgate, gives us the very word "rapture." So when we talk about the rapture, we're not inventing a term. We're using the historic language of the church to describe exactly what the text itself proclaims.

Another argument I hear is: "The early church fathers never spoke about it, so it's just a modern invention from the last hundred years." Well, I beg to differ. Clearly the apostle Paul qualifies as an early church father, and Jesus Himself is above any early church father. Both spoke vividly about the rapture throughout Scripture.

And if that weren't enough, history also shows that some early church fathers did, in fact, make statements consistent with a belief in the rapture. For example, Irenaeus (c. 130–202 AD), in *Against Heresies 5.29*, speaks of believers being "caught up" and spared from the time of tribulation. Cyprian of Carthage (c. 200–258 AD) wrote in *On the Mortality* that believers should "long for the day which assigns each of us to his own home, which snatches us hence, and sets us free from the snares of the world." Even Ephraim the Syrian (c. 306–373 AD) stated in his sermon *On the Last Times*, "All the saints and elect of God are gathered together before the tribulation, which is to come, and are taken to the LORD."

While the terminology may not always match the modern use of the word "rapture," the concept of believers being taken by Christ before the outpouring of judgment is not a new invention. It was discussed, preached, and expected among some of the earliest leaders of the church, all of whom were influenced by the apostles, and none of whom were incorrect in their assertions regarding these days, because their teaching aligned with the testimony of Scripture.

The next objection I encounter is more understandable: people simply fear it. I can relate to this one because at least they're being honest about their feelings. If they were like me, they were raised on movies like *A Thief in the Night*.

I remember struggling to fall asleep, just hearing that haunting melody in my head. No matter how cheesy that movie may have been, with the bell-bottom pants, weird music, and hippies, it was spooky. The thought of being left behind was scary. Even if you were walking with the LORD and knew Him, the thought of just being snatched up can even be frightening.

But let me explain a principle that might help you better relate to all of this. It might actually help you look forward to the rapture instead of fearing it. So let's talk about something maybe a little less fearful, like death.

Honestly, I'm not afraid of death. The idea that I'm going to die one day doesn't bother me. It used to bother me a lot, but it doesn't anymore. I know I come with an expiration date. All of us do. I think most Christians who are grounded and rooted in the Word of God aren't concerned about death. After all, according to Philippians 1:21, "For to me to live is Christ, and to die is gain."

I am a little concerned about how it's going to happen though. When it's my time, I just want to die in a blaze of glory (quickly): one moment everything's good and the next moment I'm in heaven.

I used to talk about this with my mom all the time. Not that we were worried about dying, but about how it was going to happen. So we lightheartedly made a deal that neither of us would die and that we'd both just be taken up in the rapture. There's something very peaceful about hearing the trumpet of the LORD and then in the blink of an eye being in the presence of God. There's no death involved. Quite frankly, I think that's pretty glorious.

There are people I know who are extremely Bible literate, but they're still adamant that we're not going to be taken up in the rapture prior to the tribulation. Sure, they believe the church will be raptured, but they think it's going to happen after the tribulation. I hope that when the rapture happens, the LORD lets me see the look on the faces of some of the people who were complete naysayers. Not even to hear them say "You were right," I just want to see their surprise!

Make no mistake, the rapture is without a doubt going to happen to believers. Still, there's a lot of debate about when it will occur. The Bible makes it very clear: only God knows. But I want you to understand that when God says He's going to do something, He keeps His word. You can count on it.

One benefit of paying close attention to Bible prophecy (a world I'm engulfed in): you begin to realize very quickly that God's Word is incredibly accurate. Even if it sounds completely crazy, stick to your guns, because when you hold fast to what the Bible says, eventually you come out looking like a genius.

Many of the claims I made about the Middle East, Russia, Eastern and Western Europe, and current events (particularly when they were happening) were extraordinarily unpopular. People thought I was nuts to make such statements. But knowing what the Word of God says about those regions, I'm confident that the Word of God is going to prevail, and it's going to make more sense.

Again, I want to emphasize: this is precisely why I believe all pastors should be the best geopolitical analysts in the world. If they have a thorough understanding of Bible prophecy and recognize how all the pieces fit together according to the Word of God, they'll be able to clearly discern what's happening in the world today and anticipate what could unfold in the future. For example, the constant turmoil in the Middle East, the aggression of Russia, and the growing instability across Europe all line up with the patterns Scripture has already described, reminding us that God's Word is the ultimate lens through which we interpret world events.

Here's another example of my point. Prior to 1979, when Pastor Chuck Smith (the founder of Calvary Chapel) was teaching about the aggressive actions and behavior of Iran, people called him a complete loony. They literally called him crazy. If you were born after 1979, you may find it hard to believe that Iran was a dear friend not only to the United States of America, but to Israel as well. Before then, if anyone had said Iran would become a major problem to the world, Israel, and America, they were totally dismissed. It was believed there was no way that would ever be the case.

Yet we've witnessed God completely change the geopolitics of the region. Today, the conversation about the geopolitics of the Middle East revolves around just how serious the problem of Iran is.

I even received hate mail over this issue. Many years ago, I appeared on the *Pastor's Perspective* show with Don Stewart, and they introduced me as the Middle East expert because I was from there. One question I got was, "Are you worried about ISIS? Is this a real concern for you?" My response was very simple: "I'm really not concerned about ISIS."

I made it clear to everybody that my greatest concern is Iran and what it represents (which only makes up about 3% of the Middle East population in terms of Islam). And though the Shiites are a small minority in Islam, their numbers are growing and they represent about 5% of all Islam worldwide. People thought I was crazy when I said I'm more concerned about Iran and the Shiites than I ever will be about the rest of the Arab world and the Sunnis.

I can make these assertions confidently because I know what the Bible says concerning who Iran is going to be and what they're going to be in the last days. The Bible is very clear about Iran's relationship to Eastern and Western European countries.

All that to say that the rapture will happen because God's Word says it's going to happen. It's very important that you understand the preface to all of that as we look at what's next.

The Throne Room Vision

Revelation Chapter four is a bit of an interlude, giving us details and vivid descriptions of certain things, like jewels. We shouldn't just glance over them, but I don't want to overemphasize them either. Too many Bible teachers spend considerable time focusing on what these jewels might look like and what colors they are. Let me be clear about something very important: I would never call what John saw here superfluous, nor would I ever say we should just discount it. There are some details we should think about. But I don't believe they should be the primary focus.

This chapter also reminds us that the church will be raptured before the tribulation. But perhaps the greater and more significant emphasis shows that we cannot properly function outside of the purpose for which God has created us. This becomes clear and makes a lot more sense as we get into this very critical, very powerful passage of Scripture.

Just as John gets taken up, Christians will experience the rapture in much the same way.

> "And immediately I was in the spirit: and, behold, a throne was set in heaven, and one sat on the throne."

Revelation 4:2

John is seeing a vision of God's throne. There are multiple

instances of someone in the Bible being taken before the throne of God or seeing a vision of it. Ezekiel experienced a similar vision. So did Isaiah. It's not a surprise when we read something like this.

> "And he that sat was to look upon like a jasper and a sardine stone: and there was a rainbow round about the throne, in sight like unto an emerald."
>
> **Revelation 4:3**

Now, some folks talk about the word "rainbow" used here and want to connect it to a certain alphabet movement, but there is absolutely no connection to that. What verse three describes are colors across a massive spectrum, and what John sees represents genuine beauty. It's a unique and exquisite picture.

> "And round about the throne were four and twenty seats: and upon the seats I saw four and twenty elders sitting, clothed in white raiment; and they had on their heads crowns of gold."
>
> **Revelation 4:4**

This is interesting. Many people speculate who these twenty-four elders are, and there's quite a bit of debate. J. Vernon McGee, one of the most respected Bible teachers ever, was one of the few men I've heard teach about this consistently across his entire ministry. McGee's dominant view was that this is a reference to the church. However, I respectfully disagree.

To say it's a reference to the church creates real issues, one of them being the description given by the apostle John of what he's actually seeing. Another issue is the number twenty-four, which bears significance. One possibility is it represents two covenants (the covenant made with Israel and the covenant made to the church). I don't know.

If I'm not being dogmatic about it, I could reasonably assume that twenty-four represents the result of the twelve apostles' work from which the church began and the twelve tribes of Israel. We don't know for sure and cannot make a definitive argument for who these elders are. Speculating too greatly could be dangerous. But we are certain that they are individuals of importance.

I don't think God intended for us to know who those elders were, otherwise He would have told us. But it is a very interesting conversation knowing what is coming in the future and what we have waiting for us. Although there is no way of knowing exactly who these elders are, their mention in Revelation Chapter four carries significant weight.

The picture being drawn here is one of worship, and that worship is inseparably tied to the reality of deliverance. The constraints and pains of the world have been lifted. They are gone. Those elders are no longer subject to them, and their rejoicing reflects the great deliverance of God. That picture is consequential, because it should serve as a tool to help us look forward to what awaits us.

This perspective is really important, because it shapes the way we live and act today, giving us an eternal outlook that changes our daily priorities.

"And out of the throne proceeded lightnings and thunderings and voices: and there were seven lamps of fire burning before the throne, which are the seven spirits of God."

Revelation 4:5

I have taught about this in my church (the seven spirits of God) in context with what we read in Isaiah Chapter 11. Because we see it coming up so much in Revelation, it's important to discuss it and bring emphasis to it. The seven spirits of God are vividly described in the Old Testament as being powerful and able to give us tools for living our lives for the LORD. These are very important aspects to sit with, to meditate on, and to understand. I'll say this again: as you read and understand the book of Revelation, the Old Testament is being revealed to you. That's what you're seeing. Revelation is revealing what has already existed for such a long time. Let's look at another powerful example of this right now.

> "And before the throne there was a sea of glass like unto crystal: and in the midst of the throne, and round about the throne, were four beasts full of eyes before and behind."

Revelation 4:6

The sea of glass depicted here is powerful, especially if you know the Old Testament and understand ancient culture. In Bible times, the sea was the last frontier, enormous, powerful, and untamed. It was something most people feared.

This sea of glass surrounding the throne of God illustrates something people cannot tame, yet it is completely under God's control. And at the same time, the fact that He has total control over what's around him increases the reverent fear that humanity has of the true and living God. He rests above everything that is tumultuous or ominous with total authority.

In a much smaller way, this principle plays out in my home. We have a Labradoodle puppy who's very cute, smart, and picks up on things quickly, yet he's everything you'd expect in a puppy. He sleeps a lot, then suddenly wakes up and loses his mind. Like all dogs, he's a pack animal, and he knows I'm the "alpha" (the guy who means business in the house).

When we leave and no one is home, we put him in his crate. He barks nonstop and will not shut up. I get it, he's basically saying, "I don't like being in this crate. Let me out." When we return home and my wife, Nicole, walks in, it sounds like there are fifteen dogs barking. But when I walk in? That puppy doesn't make a peep. He even recognizes my footsteps and doesn't even breathe heavily.

Why? Because even though he's only been in our home a few months, he's figured out that if Nicole hears him barking like crazy, he might get attention and be let out of his crate sooner. But when I walk in and he starts barking, he's going to hear "Shhh!" I don't let him out and reward him for making noise. The puppy understands this. If he gets too excited and plays aggressively, all I have to do is look at him and he calms down.

My little children think their Dad has some kind of weird super power, and they're in awe of the whole thing. But even our little puppy instinctively understands what authority is and who's in control.

When John describes the throne of God surrounded by the sea, he uses the very image of the sea, something humanity has always feared and continues to fear. Yet here, that sea is so completely submitted to God that it appears like glass. This points us back to moments in the Old Testament where God demonstrated his power over the waters: when He parted the Red Sea so Israel could cross on dry ground, or when Elijah struck the Jordan River and it was divided so he and Elisha could pass through. These accounts remind us that God has always had complete authority over what people fear.

The imagery in Revelation carries the same truth, showing that Almighty God has absolute control over everything we could possibly fear. If you learn to see God in that same way, you can substitute the sea for whatever your greatest fear may be. You'll be able to face it and say, "Okay, I understand. I know who I'm dealing with here. God is in control." And it's that very reality that should lead every one of us to walk in the reverent fear of the LORD.

I want to mention that I'm not fond of the King James translation here. It's not the translation itself that bothers me, it's the Elizabethan English. Some words sound strange or even misleading to modern readers, not because the translators got it wrong, but because English from that era carried different meanings than they do today. Take the word "terrible," for example. The King James version often uses it when the true meaning is closer to "awesome" or "awe-inspiring." That shift in language can confuse some readers.

> "...and in the midst of the throne, and round about the throne, were four beasts full of eyes before and behind."

Revelation 4:6

What it should say is "four living creatures." That's a more accurate term, in my opinion. When most people read the word "beast," they picture demons or some monster lurking around the throne. Add in the description of these four living creatures, and it sounds even more ominous. But that's not what's happening here. What we're about to read in verse seven is a description of the cherubim. We see something similar in Ezekiel and Isaiah. It's important to understand that this passage is a reiteration of those earlier visions.

> "And the first beast was like a lion, and the second beast like a calf, and the third beast had a face as a man, and the fourth beast was like a flying eagle."

Revelation 4:7

This is really fascinating! When you think about how these living creatures are described, it clearly mirrors the attributes of Christ. But please, don't confuse these creatures with Christ himself.

However, notice:

- One was like a lion (as in the Lion of Judah).
- One was like a calf (as something sacrificial).
- One had the face of a man (as Jesus shared in our humanity).
- One was like an eagle (for those who wait on him, they're carried on wings like an eagle).

These living creatures are cherubim, and this description paints a picture of a unique and powerful God who sits on the throne.

> "And the four beasts had each of them six wings about him; and they were full of eyes within: and they rest not day and night, saying, Holy, holy, holy, LORD God Almighty, which was, and is, and is to come."

Revelation 4:8

When most people read the passage "Holy, holy, holy is the LORD God Almighty. He was, He is, and He is to come," they think of the famous hymn and move on. But if you pause and consider what's actually written here, it's remarkable.

Let's look at it through a scientific lens, starting with Einstein's general theory of relativity. This theory explains that time functions as a dimension, woven together with the three spatial dimensions into a single fabric called spacetime. In general relativity, time doesn't pass at a fixed rate. It's affected by both an observer's speed and by the curvature of spacetime caused by mass. A hundred and fifty years ago, this would have been dismissed as nonsense. But today, thanks to our understanding of physics, we know this is true. Time really is a dimension, and God sits outside of it. Do you understand what that means? He's watching the beginning of everything at the same time He's watching what we're reading about in Revelation. He sees it all simultaneously, not as a linear timeline the way we do.

So when we read about God (who is, who was, and is to come), it means He is present in all of those moments simultaneously. When Jesus says, "Before Abraham was, I am," that's exactly what he's referring to. He sits outside of time. Now that's a pretty spectacular picture. These angels understand this too, as they worship God.

> "And when those beasts give glory and honor and thanks to him that sat on the throne, who liveth for ever and ever."

Revelation 4:9

I want to call out something happening in this verse that's deeply relevant to our lives here on earth. The angels are doing what we'll eventually do for eternity: glorifying and giving thanks to God. But there's more to it than that. They never grow tired or weary in glorifying God because they were created specifically for worship. We know God created everyone with a purpose, and when we live outside that purpose, life can become pretty miserable. But when we live out the purpose God created us for, we discover true fulfillment and joy.

> "The four and twenty elders fall down before him that sat on the throne, and worship him that liveth for ever and ever, and cast their crowns before the throne, saying, Thou art worthy, O LORD, to receive glory and honour and power: for thou hast created all things, and for thy pleasure they are and were created."

Revelation 4:10-11

Wow! Did you get that? If you've ever wondered what the purpose of life is, there's your answer right there. God created you for His pleasure. Now, some might think that sounds strange or even sadistic, that God would create mankind for His pleasure. What kind of God does that? A God who loves you. A generous and relational Creator who wants to give you the absolute best of everything from within Himself.

God wants you to experience a purposeful, fulfilling life beyond anything you can possibly imagine. Consider the alternative: when people reject God and refuse to live according to His purpose and will, they choose eternity separated from Him, experiencing the consequences of their sin in hell.

All the misery we see in our world is rooted in mankind's choice to live outside of God's intended purpose. There is only one true God of the universe. He is holy and good, and He lovingly created you for His pleasure so that in Him you will have an abundant and everlasting life.

Living for God's Pleasure: The Key to Life

If you're like most parents, you'll understand how this concept relates. My wife and I once had to create a consequence for a very specific behavior my daughter exhibited. We made it crystal clear: "If you do this particular thing, you won't be allowed to participate in something very special we had planned." As a father, I live for the moments when I see that extraordinary smile on my daughter's face as she experiences fun things. As parents, we love watching our children be happy, which makes it painful when they don't listen and do the things we ask them to do, because we know consequences must follow. From a child's perspective, it might seem like, "Mom and Dad don't want me to have fun. They just want to make life miserable for me." But children don't always understand that their parents make rules because they want them to live in a safe, healthy, and joyful environment. In reality, parents want their children to experience every wonderful thing that's meant for them.

In the same way, God says "I created you for a purpose,

and that purpose is to do My will. And if you choose to live outside of that purpose, you'll be miserable." It's no coincidence that in recent years we've seen an unprecedented rise in suicidal ideation and self-harm. Historically high numbers of children committing crimes are being reported. At times, it appears we're watching society collapse in ways we've never seen before. It's shocking to witness, but it shouldn't come as a surprise. Our culture centers around instant gratification and easy access to every amenity and pleasure people have created. Yet the world is becoming more desperate, more hostile, more frustrated, and more isolated. Why? Because people are not living according to the purpose and calling God has set forth for them.

Here's the thing: if you're struggling to find joy and happiness right now, you will not find it by chasing what the world offers to give you. You won't find it in wealth or social media followers. You won't find it in a promotion at work. You won't find it spending every weekend at your kids' sports games. You won't even find it by going to church every time the doors open or participating in every church social event.

The only way to find what your heart longs for is to look to God, understand the purpose He designed you for, and live for His pleasure. When we walk according to God's will, our lives become fuller and happier, even amid persecution, difficulty, and hardship. Despite the pain and suffering we often experience in the world, the Bible says Christians can "count it all joy." Paul encouraged us with these words:

> "For I reckon that the sufferings of this present time are not worthy to be compared with the glory which

shall be revealed in us."

Romans 8:18

The better we get at worshiping the true and living God, the more fulfilling our lives become. It's absolutely true. Your life is most meaningful and joyful when you live according to God's plan and purposes for you.

5

Who Is Worthy?

As we continue, the Apostle John describes not only heaven but also the throne of God. At this point, we know for sure based on what we read in Revelation Chapter 1 that we're now in a future place. What we're about to read hasn't happened yet. Let me say it again: you'll be able to understand the Book of Revelation if you understand the Old Testament. I emphasize this because the more you know about what's been established in the Old Testament, the easier it is to recognize those patterns and prophecies in Revelation.

This is why I'm genuinely thankful you're reading this book. If you haven't already noticed, one of my primary goals in writing it is to help you better understand the Old Testament as a foundation for understanding Revelation. My hope is that, as we go through this together, you'll begin to see how the two are inseparably connected, and how your grasp of one deepens your appreciation and comprehension of the other.

I was at a memorial service recently, and thankfully it was a joyful celebration, because there was no doubt this man was with the LORD. We remembered our dear brother and celebrated that he was with Jesus. It's pretty remarkable to think he's experiencing the wonder of heaven just as John wrote about. He's watching it, seeing it, and receiving the reward for the life he lived. I stopped for a moment and reflected on the power of God's salvation, and honestly, I almost envied where he is right now. I didn't even look at his casket because I wanted my last memory of him on earth to be our last conversation. But I rejoiced because he's in heaven with the LORD, in the place we all long to be.

John has just finished describing heaven and the throne of God. The church has already been raptured, and now we're stepping into a fascinating scenario, one that's hard to grasp without understanding the cultures and laws of ancient Bible times. Let's walk through it together and make sense of it all.

The Sealed Scroll

"And I saw in the right hand of Him that sat on the throne a book written within and on the backside, sealed with seven seals."

Revelation 5:1

We should note that books as we know them today, with binding and pages, are a relatively modern invention. Books like we have today didn't exist in Bible times. Instead, they used scrolls: one long page made of papyrus or animal skin. You'd hold the scroll horizontally and use your right hand to unroll the text column by column. The ancient scroll containing the Book of Revelation would have been about twenty feet long. So when you see the word "book," think "scroll."

Notice in verse one that there are seven seals on this scroll.

That number seven represents "completion." Although I'm not a big fan of biblical numerology, there is a reason God brings these numbers to our attention. It's important to understand that we're talking about something "final." The seven seals on this scroll emphasize that we're establishing something with permanence, with real finality.

Although the devil continues trying to minimize God's Word by distracting people from its truth, we know that when God makes a declaration, it's unmovable and permanent. God's Word changes our hearts, but the Word itself never changes. The scroll sealed with seven seals isn't just permanent, it's closed and can't be opened.

The Title Deed to the Earth

Now this gets really interesting.

> "And I saw a strong angel proclaiming with a loud voice, Who is worthy to open the book, and to loose the seals thereof?"
>
> **Revelation 5:2**

The questions often asked about Revelation Chapter 5 are: "What does this scroll represent? What makes it so central to this portion of Revelation?" I need to give you a spoiler alert here because it's important.

I believe it's the title deed to the earth.

This can be difficult to grasp if you're unfamiliar with ancient cultures. Back in ancient Bible times, the way families operated was critical to preserving multiple generations. I wish families still worked this way.

What I'm about to describe is built upon God's original intention for mankind, expressed through the commands He gave Adam and Eve. In Genesis Chapter 1, He gave five commands to them and said, "Be fruitful, and multiply, and replenish the earth, and subdue it: and have dominion over the fish of the sea, and over the fowl of the air, and over every living thing that moveth upon the earth."

Each command was rooted in God's intention for Adam and Eve to be fruitful in the most abundant and beautiful environment any human being has ever known. They were to build their family enterprise by giving each generation an apportionment of the land that had already been given to them. Essentially, the original family compound they were meant to establish was the garden itself, the entirety of what mankind knew of the earth at that time.

The patriarchal family structure that exists today isn't a curse word; it was God's design for mankind. With every generation fulfilling those original five commands, there was meant to be growth building upon the foundation God provided to the family. When we revisit what we see in Revelation regarding the title deed of the earth being reclaimed by God to be given back to His people, it becomes clear how foundational this truth really is. As I've mentioned several times, Genesis was the beginning, and Revelation is the end, which in essence becomes the gateway into eternity itself.

When Israel went into the land of the Philistines and defeated their enemies, they were apportioned land. Each tribe was given a massive piece of land, and each family in that tribe was given a portion of that land. Back then, if you had a piece of land, you weren't talking about an acre or two, which would be extremely valuable today in places like Manhattan or the California coast. You were sometimes looking at square miles. We're talking about a lot of land.

If you were the father who originally received this piece of land, you built a home there. This is where you raised your children and built a farm. When your children grew up, they built homes on that same piece of land, and eventually you'd have a compound, because your children, their children, and their children would all build there, generation after generation. Your family would contribute to the same farm, grow it, expand the family business, start ranching, or do anything else that would grow the family enterprise.

In the Middle Eastern culture I grew up in, we don't leave the house until we get married. Until then, you contribute to the household. If you were a female, this was particularly important because the family around you acted as your covering until you came into your new covering, your husband. When that happened, your new family would be covered as a unit by the older generations. If you were a young man, this was equally important because it provided a launching pad for you to step into the responsibility of becoming a covering yourself. The infrastructure around you gave you everything you needed to walk into the role God called you to as a husband, a father, and the spiritual covering for your new family. This is why you don't leave your family's household until you get married. This infrastructure designed by God was critical for learning to contribute like an adult, taking on financial responsibility, and using the arrangement for financial advantages like investing and saving. In ancient times, the idea is, you wouldn't move away. Even when you left your parents' house, you'd build a new house on that land. It would someday become a larger compound, and eventually those compounds turned into cities.

Sometimes, families faced extraordinarily difficult situations and were forced to sell their land to survive. When this happened, it was customary to make an agreement with the new owner that would allow the family to continue living on and working the land, even though they'd sold it. This arrangement benefited the new property owner, but it almost always included a loophole: the family could buy back their land within a year, or in some cases, seven years. That was the rule.

These agreements were clearly written and documented on a scroll. Every detail was covered: the land's borders, the terms of the agreement, and what was necessary to regain possession. It was essentially a sales contract. Once the agreement was written on the scroll, it was sealed to show the transaction was complete. The only way to reclaim your land was to fulfill the obligations in the agreement. Then and only then did you earn the right to claim the scroll back. Once the new landowner was repaid, he'd return the scroll to the family, who would break the seals and restore ownership of the land back to themselves.

With that in mind, and assuming the scroll in Revelation 5:1 is the title deed to the earth, the next two verses make sense. Look what happens:

No One Found Worthy

"And no man in heaven, nor in earth, neither under the earth, was able to open the book, neither to look thereon. And I wept much, because no man was found worthy to open and to read the book, neither to look thereon."

Revelation 5:3–4

I believe John weeps for several reasons, all deeply rooted in the first three chapters of Genesis. Let's start with the obvious: John realizes the deadline to reclaim the title deed to the earth has passed. In heaven, the scroll is sitting there and there's no one to open it. No one has met the requirements to take back possession of the earth. John grasps the existential weight of this moment. Imagine what he's feeling. He's watching over people he's cared for, always hoping the Creator would redeem the world again, and he sees that no one in heaven or on earth can claim the scroll. He's likely thinking the world will remain forever doomed, controlled by wickedness.

How would you feel if, despite all the wickedness in the world today, you had no hope that things could get better? Would you even be motivated to act? I do what I do every day because God called me to it, and I carry hope in my heart that by His grace, things will change. I fight for our country because I believe God, in His infinite grace and mercy, might grant us a reprieve. I do it because God tells me to. That's the reason we should all be doing the same thing.

Let me give you a couple of caveats here so we can understand this correctly. One of the reasons we can see why John was deeply affected by this is because he was processing events through the lens of early biblical history. We know from Genesis that when God created the earth, it belonged to Him. But God did something remarkable after creating the heavens and the earth. He created mankind, and as Genesis 1:27 says, He created us in His likeness and in His image. As I mentioned earlier, God commanded us to take what He had given us, this earth, and do five specific things with it: be fruitful, multiply, replenish the earth, subdue it, and have dominion over everything.

The problem was that man wasn't satisfied with what he'd been given. Instead of focusing on all that was entrusted to him, man fixated on the one thing he didn't have: the fruit God had forbidden him from eating. That became the central issue. Adam chose to rebel against God and eat the fruit, and in doing so, he forfeited the title deed of the earth that had been given to him. That title deed then passed into Satan's possession.

We know this because later in the Gospels, when Satan tempted Jesus, he offered Him what amounted to the title deed of the world (Luke 4:5–7). Notice that Jesus didn't dispute Satan's claim of ownership. Instead, He responded on an entirely different level, affirming God's ultimate authority. So when John witnesses this scene in Revelation, he's recognizing that same reality. Satan still possesses the earth, and the scroll with the seals represents that title deed.

What makes this moment even more critical is John's deep awareness of humanity's condition. He certainly knew Paul's teaching that through one man, sin entered into the world. But frankly, John didn't need Paul's letters to grasp this truth. His own writings show he understood it completely. Because of Adam's fall, all humanity was born into total depravity, and healing couldn't come until the perfect Lamb of God accomplished His redemptive work and took away the world's sins. Yet even with God's provision of salvation through His Son, Jesus Christ, redemption wouldn't be complete without restoring humanity's rightful possession of the earth, fulfilling God's original plan for our eternal home. So when John stands in heaven in the last days, looking at the future, and sees that no one can redeem the scroll, you can imagine the hopelessness that overwhelms him. What he doesn't yet see is that the scroll is about to be redeemed, signifying the restoration of earth's rightful ownership and the return of hope as God originally intended.

The Bible makes it clear that John wept bitterly. Why? Because he understood the devastating loss that would result. In that moment, John realized that if no one could take up that scroll, the whole world would continue down its path of evil, growing darker and darker. That would be such a hopeless feeling, understanding just how dark this world is becoming.

The Lion of the Tribe of Judah

"And one of the elders saith unto me, Weep not: behold, the Lion of the tribe of Judah, the Root of David, hath prevailed to open the book, and to loose the seven seals thereof."

Revelation 5:5

Reading this makes me want to cry.

The Lion of the tribe of Judah, Jesus is the only One who could step up to open that scroll. He paid an enormous price for the world. The world was His because He created it. Then it was taken from the people He gave it to. But to reclaim what

He created, Jesus had to pay for it, and the price He paid was staggering.

What we see in Revelation 5:5 is that Christ is identified as the only One worthy to take the scroll and open it. That truth is so powerful and substantial, and it gives us hope for the future.

Look what it goes on to say:

"And I beheld, and, lo, in the midst of the throne and of the four beasts, and in the midst of the elders, stood a Lamb as it had been slain, having seven horns and seven eyes, which are the seven spirits of God sent forth into all the earth."

Revelation 5:6

Let's look at the seven horns and the seven eyes. Seven is the number of complete and total fullness. The horn was a symbol of power. So if Jesus had seven horns, it means He has complete power. And we know what the eyes represent. Eyes speak of seeing and knowing, because what you see is what you know. So if you have seven eyes, you have a complete perspective on everything. This speaks to the fact that Christ is all-knowing, all-seeing, and all-powerful. He's the One. He's everything. He's the One going back to claim the title deed.

By the way, I believe another reason John was crying his eyes out was because he was seeing Christ in His crucified state. Only people in the military and law enforcement, or doctors and nurses, will be able to relate to this. But there's a certain point in your career when you get numb to seeing death, it just doesn't affect you as much. But if you're not accustomed to death and you see someone who has been critically injured, your instant reaction is to turn away.

The Bible tells us that when Christ was crucified, His appearance was so horrific that people couldn't bear to look at Him. I believe John is seeing Jesus in that scarred state and probably turns away because he can't stand the sight. It must have brought back the terrible memory of watching Jesus die on the cross, because if you remember, John was at the crucifixion with Mary, witnessing the entire horrific scene.

What's striking is that John connects the omniscience of God, the omnipotence of God, the Almighty Himself, with those wounds and scars. Isaiah 53 describes this and it's pretty amazing. No wonder John is overwhelmed by what he's seeing.

The Lamb Takes the Scroll

"And He came and took the book out of the right hand of Him that sat upon the throne."

Revelation 5:7

"And when He had taken the book, the four beasts and four and twenty elders fell down before the Lamb, having every one of them harps, and golden vials full of odours, which are the prayers of the saints."

Revelation 5:8

The reference to "vials full of odors" creates a powerful connection to Old Testament imagery. This principle comes alive in Exodus, Leviticus, and Numbers through the sacrifices offered in the tabernacle. Each offering made by the children of Israel represented more than obedience and worship, it symbolized fellowship with God through prayer and petition. Every sacrifice burning on the altar was symbolic of the prayers of the saints ascending to heaven, just as the smoke from those offerings rose upward before the LORD.

Exodus 29:18 says, "And thou shalt burn the whole ram upon the altar: it is a burnt offering unto the LORD: it is a sweet savour, an offering made by fire unto the LORD." The fragrance of the sacrifice symbolized the pleasure and acceptance of God toward the prayers and worship of His people.

Leviticus reinforces this truth repeatedly. In Leviticus 2:2 we read, "And he shall bring it to Aaron's sons the priests: and he shall take there out his handful of the flour thereof, and of the oil thereof, with all the frankincense thereof; and the priest shall burn the memorial of it upon the altar, to be an offering made by fire, of a sweet savour unto the LORD."

Similarly, Numbers 15:3 says, "And will make an offering by fire unto the LORD, a burnt offering, or a sacrifice in performing a vow, or in a freewill offering, or in your solemn feasts, to make a sweet savour unto the LORD, of the herd, or of the flock." Just as the offering in the tabernacle rose as a sweet-smelling savour to the LORD, our prayers ascend before His throne today. The symbolism remains unchanged: the fragrance represents our heart and intent as we worship Him, showing us how precious our prayers are to God. He receives them as something beautiful, sacred, and deeply pleasing to Him, just as we see in Revelation 5:8.

God keeps every prayer we have ever offered to Him. Understand, not only does God value our prayers and hold them dearly to His heart, but He also answers them. And when God opens up the seals, something remarkable happens.

> "And they sung a new song, saying, Thou art worthy to take the book, and to open the seals thereof: for Thou wast slain, and hast redeemed us to God by thy blood out of every kindred, and tongue, and people, and nation; And hast made us unto our God kings and priests: and we shall reign on the earth."
>
> **Revelation 5:9–10**

By the way, this is where I deeply disagree with some modern translations. Some change Revelation 5:10 to read, "He has made them unto our God." That's wrong. I understand the argument, there's a textual variance in the Greek manuscripts, but contextually and grammatically, the correct word is "us," not "them." Even if you interpret it as "them," the context still demands we read it as "us."

The exciting part is this: He has made us kings and priests unto our God. We're going to reign and rule with Him on earth. Isn't that exciting? God's doing something for us, and it's going to happen during the millennial reign of Christ.

The Heavenly Worship

> "And I beheld, and I heard the voice of many angels round about the throne and the beasts and the elders: and the number of them was ten thousand times ten thousand, and thousands of thousands."
>
> **Revelation 5:11**

This is incredible to consider. The sheer power of an angel

is staggering. In 2 Kings 19:35, we read that an angel, acting as God's agent, killed 185,000 elite Assyrian soldiers overnight while they besieged Jerusalem during King Hezekiah's reign. Now think about all the angels out there doing what they do. With many angels around the throne, just imagine the power represented in that room. And this is what they say, notice the next verses:

> "Saying with a loud voice, Worthy is the Lamb that was slain to receive power, and riches, and wisdom, and strength, and honour, and glory, and blessing."
>
> **Revelation 5:12**
>
> "And every creature which is in heaven, and on the earth, and under the earth, and such as are in the sea, and all that are in them, heard I saying, Blessing, and honour, and glory, and power, be unto Him that sitteth upon the throne, and unto the Lamb for ever and ever."
>
> **Revelation 5:13**
>
> "And the four beasts said, Amen. And the four and twenty elders fell down and worshiped Him that liveth for ever and ever."
>
> **Revelation 5:14**

When you say "amen," it means "so be it." It's final.

I often tell people who don't know the LORD, not to be harsh, but because they need to hear the truth: "You will one day declare Jesus Christ as LORD." Let me be clear. We can go back and forth all day on intellectually-based arguments. We can discuss linguistics, science, and every aspect of what we read in Scripture. But here's what you need to know; it will happen.

The problem is this: if you wait until you're forced to declare it, you're going to hell. You can fight it all you want, but if you wait too long, the consequences will be devastating. Your hard heart will have already destroyed your life. But if you choose to follow the LORD now, you'll be so grateful you did. The reward that awaits is so incredible. You have no idea.

The Victory Is Assured

Folks, here's the joy and peace we get to walk in. After reading about the encounter John describes, it's abundantly clear: God wins. This is incredible. As dark as things get, as terrible as they are, God will come out victorious!

Because I know the result, it's so much easier to fight. Get out there and fight the good fight. Just go for it! Swing harder than you ever have before. Do the work God has called you to do. It's critical. It's important. We're not doing it because we think we can make a difference in our own strength. We do it so God may have mercy on our nation. He is able to make a difference. And we do it because God's called us to, because He is faithful and good.

Here's my encouragement to you: Stay close to the LORD. Walk in purity. Don't waste your time on things that don't matter. Serve God with your whole heart and watch Him do amazing things. Time is running out. We don't know how much is left, so take advantage of it. Amen.

6
The First Four Seals

When it comes to geopolitics, government structures, the different types of rulers that emerge, or the history of governments (anything socially based like this), Christians should be the best in their understanding of these infrastructures. In fact, pastors should be the foremost experts in geopolitics, whether it's the regional dynamics of the Middle East or the global political landscape as it relates to Bible prophecy. Why? Because if they truly know the Bible and understand what it says about the future, they are going to clearly understand everything about the geopolitical forces at work in the Bible.

From the outset, I want to be clear: understanding Bible prophecy doesn't just make us the best geopolitical analysts alive, but it also equips us to understand the sociological constructs that shape how political systems actually move and function. Many people say politics don't belong in the church, but I can't think of a more incorrect statement. If you have a biblical worldview, you'll understand that politics, in essence, flows from the pulpit. Politics, by definition, is the expression of what's sociologically established through how people interact within their communities. God has called us to step into the public square, and He hasn't called us to do it empty-handed. He's given us the ultimate tools to understand the heart and mind of man: the Holy Spirit who lives within us and the guidance of His Word. These empower us to discern how morality should be legislated and to recognize the core of our greatest sociological failures. Here's a simple truth that will help you walk among the most brilliant diagnosticians alive: when you see these failures, they're the direct result of walking away from God's commands. What we're about to see in the next few verses will demonstrate this reality in a way that's both eye-opening and sobering.

The Stage Is Set

We're living in the last days, and the world around us is changing rapidly. You're not going to believe how quickly we witness this stuff unfold. When I say unfold, I'm not talking about watching the seals of Revelation breaking right now, but we are watching the world's stage being set to put all of this in place.

For example, the level of hatred against Jews that we're witnessing right now around the world is unlike anything we've seen before. I'd even venture to say it's far worse than anything we witnessed during World War II, which is terrifying for several reasons. First and foremost, because it acts as a destructive force that consumes anyone who allows themselves to become preoccupied by it. We know for a fact that in the last days we will see an increase in hatred against Jews, and we see evidence of this in Zechariah, which says,

> "And in that day will I make Jerusalem a burdensome stone for all people: all that burden themselves with

it shall be cut in pieces, though all the people of the earth be gathered together against it."

Zechariah 12:3

We also see this same pattern prophesied concerning the hatred and persecution of Christians, as Paul writes:

"Yea, and all that will live godly in Christ Jesus shall suffer persecution."

2 Timothy 3:12

And by the way, I need to emphasize that the context of 2 Timothy 3:12 sits directly on Paul's declaration at the beginning of the chapter, where he speaks about the last days. So we know beyond a shadow of a doubt that we're talking about the end times. Right now, we're seeing both of these increase exponentially in ways never before seen in human history.

We are undoubtedly in the last days. As we approach them, we should be excited knowing that we're not going to be in the midst of any of that nonsense. God is going to rapture us. What's amazing about all of this is understanding the extraordinary things that God has waiting for us. Things that are truly exciting.

The Foundation of Understanding

Now, before we dive into the seals, I need to answer a question I get asked all the time: Are we witnessing the Four Horsemen of Revelation Chapter 6 right now? Are we actually watching the first four seals unfold before our eyes?

No, we're not (refer to my comments on Revelation 1:19). But here's something crucial I want you to understand: What we read in Revelation Chapter 6 will happen after we are raptured, not necessarily during the tribulation. Some of the seals we see here will be opened just before the tribulation begins.

> "And I saw when the Lamb opened one of the seals, and I heard, as it were the noise of thunder, one of the four beasts saying, Come and see."
>
> **Revelation 6:1**
>
> "And I saw, and behold a white horse: and he that sat on him had a bow; and a crown was given unto him: and he went forth conquering, and to conquer."
>
> **Revelation 6:2**

The first seal we see here is the rider on the white horse; the final Antichrist. Here's the key issue: the tribulation can't begin until the final Antichrist is revealed to the world and confirms the covenant described in Daniel 9:27. Since the first seal is the rider of the white horse (the Antichrist), this seal must be broken before the tribulation starts.

This creates confusion because it happens after the rapture. I don't believe this seal breaks during the tribulation. Instead, I think it breaks just before the tribulation begins, since the final Antichrist kicks things off by strengthening that covenant.

Now, even though we are not witnessing these events firsthand (because we haven't been raptured yet), I want you to understand something important: God uses these end times scenarios in Revelation to reflect a pattern we've seen throughout human history. Yes, this is a future event that will definitely happen, but there's a pattern within the first four seals that we need to recognize.

The first four seals in Revelation Chapter 6 are what I call man-made seals. These are judgments poured out on mankind as a direct result of humanity's sinful actions.

The Pattern of Destruction

Let me explain something about the spirit of Antichrist, because we need to understand this. The spirit of Antichrist has been here forever. For thousands of years, we've seen it at work around us. When we talk about the spirit of Antichrist, understand that "anti" doesn't mean "against." The term comes from the Greek prefix ἀντί (anti), which in classical and Koine Greek primarily means "in place of" or "instead of." While it can sometimes convey opposition, its deeper meaning points to substitution or replacement. In other words, the Antichrist isn't simply someone who stands against Christ, but someone who seeks to replace Him, positioning himself as a counterfeit Messiah to take Christ's place in worship and authority. So when we talk about the spirit of Antichrist, we're talking about a spirit that's been around for a long time, influencing mankind. It seeks to remove the collective consciousness of God by actually assuming God's role.

We're seeing this happen in governments all over the world, in many different ways. We're seeing it happen in society. The spirit of Antichrist is exactly that: a mentality that says we're going to replace God by assuming His role, solely with the intent to remove God from people's minds.

This is what happens when totalitarian rulers seize power. They try to replace the true and living God. They demand the worship that belongs only to Him, under the guise of some revolutionary cause. They manufacture a terrible crisis to instill fear in the very people they claim to protect. When people buy the lie and give in to that fear, they adopt a totalitarian mindset and follow a path of destruction that ruins lives.

This is why you'll often hear me use the term "final Antichrist." I use it because there have been many antichrists throughout history, just as John tells us:

> "Little children, it is the last time: and as ye have heard that antichrist shall come, even now are there many antichrists; whereby we know that it is the last time."
>
> **1 John 2:18**

But the final Antichrist is the one who will rise to global prominence during the tribulation period, and he will be the most consequential of them all. When you look at the final Antichrist, you need to understand that he will be the most destructive human being who has ever lived. What makes him truly unique is that he'll operate in a time when he's completely unchecked, because Christians will not be alive on this earth. We will have been raptured.

At the risk of sounding redundant, let me reiterate: we've seen many antichrists in the past. Many people have embodied the spirit of Antichrist and could very well have been used by the devil to become the Antichrist. But God's timing is always perfect. Throughout human history, these antichrists have shown their ugly faces in every context. Yet because of the presence of Christians, these antichrists have never been able to reach their full potential.

Some of you might say, "Well, James, that's kind of scary if you think about it. Some of the rulers who existed during World War II took so many lives. It's hard to imagine it getting much worse." It can, and it will.

Hitler was a prime example of this. If you study the record of totalitarian rulers, you'll see that the majority of the most effective and destructive leaders originated in Western Europe Why? Because the devil has tried to raise up individuals who would be the perfect candidates to be possessed by him and function as that final Antichrist. But all of this is subject to God's timeline and His schedule.

It's also important to understand that as long as Christians are here on earth doing the job we're supposed to be doing, while filled with the Spirit of God and standing against unrighteousness, then we know that evil will never come to complete fruition. We act as that restraining force. We see this in 2 Thessalonians Chapter 2.

The Restraining Force Removed

What I believe keeps the world from completely imploding the way it seems to be doing right now centers around the fact that Christians are here. The Bible tells us that as believers, we are the preserving influence on society.

Things haven't become as deeply evil as they could be because believers filled with the Spirit of God are still here. This is a crucial point for us to understand. Because once we begin to dig into what the world will look like when Christians are actually gone, the picture becomes grim. It's really, really bad. Consider this: totalitarian rule alone has killed roughly 300 million people in the last 150 years. That's like the entire population of America suddenly dying. That's the death toll of totalitarian rule.

But the following verses show us what totalitarian rule looks like when Christians are removed from the earth. The result may be anywhere from three to four billion people lost almost immediately. Think about that for a second. That's the difference Christians make when we stand up and fight for the truth.

The Four Horsemen Revealed

When we read about the first four seals in the Book of Revelation, they reveal a timeless pattern of totalitarian rule. We'll look at the riders of the white horse, the red horse, the black horse, and the pale horse. Each of them represents something unique.

The White Horse: The Final Antichrist

"And I saw when the Lamb opened one of the seals, and I heard, as it were the noise of thunder, one of the four beasts saying, Come and see. And I saw, and behold a white horse: and he that sat on him had a bow; and a crown was given unto him: and he went forth conquering, and to conquer."

Revelation 6:1–2

The white horse represents the ultimate totalitarian ruler, Satan himself, the Antichrist. This person will physically be here on earth. Quite frankly, he might be living among us right now. We just haven't met him yet, and he hasn't been revealed to us.

Notice some important details about this rider. The text says he had a bow, and a crown was given to him. But here's what's striking: he had a bow without an arrow. And that crown? It was given to him. This means he's an influential and powerful ruler who will scare people into full and complete submission with his words alone, not by actually deploying the weapon that would cause people to comply.

In many cases, it won't even be through fear. In fact, most of the time it's going to be through flattery. "I can give you the hope you've been looking for." Remember, the Jews during this time period think this is their Messiah. They're going to realize very quickly, at the Revelation Chapter 13 mark, that he isn't the Messiah at all, and they've made a terrible mistake. They're going to back off and wonder, "What in the world did we do?" They're going to repent and then become some of the most extraordinary people and evangelists on earth at that time.

This guy will have a crown, meaning he's a ruler. And he has a bow but no arrow. What does the Bible say? He's a conqueror who pretty much rules everything. There will be a confederation of nations that comes out of Europe, which is already forming right now, and they're going to yield their power to one person who will rule furiously.

The Red Horse: War Unleashed

Now look what happens in verses three and four:

"And when he had opened the second seal, I heard the second beast say, Come and see. And there went out another horse that was red: and power was given to him that sat thereon to take peace from the earth, and that they should kill one another: and there was given unto him a great sword."

Revelation 6:3–4

The Bible says the rider of this red horse will take away peace. What's coming is full-scale war. If you want to get a glimpse of what this is going to look like in the last days, look at Ukraine right now. President Volodymyr Zelenskyy (their totalitarian ruler, wicked as he is) works against peace and throws away every opportunity to make it.

We promised Russia during the Gorbachev era that we wouldn't expand NATO. And what happened? Our elected leaders pushed to expand NATO further and further. Some people might say, "Well, James, what's the big deal about expanding NATO?" Because, as NATO expanded (or our government's aggressive rhetoric ramped up), it threatened Russia's ability to maintain its sovereignty.

These facts have caused me to deeply despise the war-embracing sentiment we're seeing from certain members of the Republican Party. The terrible reality is that the discussion about NATO expansion was fueled by several members of the Republican Party. I don't need to mention names to tell you that many senior members were calling for Putin's assassination before Russia ever went into Ukraine. The large-scale death we've seen in both countries was directly caused by that.

If you want to get a picture of what this red horse who takes peace away looks like, just look at what's happening in Ukraine right now. There's a very concerted effort to destroy anything that even remotely resembles peace. Is it a coincidence that Zelenskyy, who right now is the totalitarian ruler of Ukraine, has been killing priests left and right? Is it a coincidence that he's killing his political opponents?

I predicted this would happen, and many people called me crazy. Zelenskyy also did exactly what we knew was coming. He basically said, "I'm delaying or stopping elections. We're not having any elections right now because we're at war."

I also think it's important to offer another caveat here. My statements on this matter shouldn't be conflated with any kind of allegiance to Vladimir Putin, because the Russian president has shown many open demonstrations of totalitarian rule as well. I'm simply using the discussion surrounding these matters to provide an active demonstration of how the passage we're discussing applies today.

Think about it: the first thing totalitarian rulers do is introduce war into the picture. War becomes the excuse to build their empire. It's the tool they use to hold onto power use to carry out all the evil things you want to do.

The white horse comes first (this final Antichrist comes in). Then the red horse comes brings the war that ends all wars.

The Black Horse: Economic Collapse

"And when he had opened the third seal, I heard the third beast say, Come and see. And I beheld, and lo a black horse; and he that sat on him had a pair of balances in his hand. And I heard a voice in the midst of the four beasts say, A measure of wheat for a penny, and three measures of barley for a penny; and see thou hurt not the oil and the wine."

Revelation 6:5–6

When war erupts, terrible famine sweeps across the land, followed by economic collapse, leading to rapid inflation.

I remember when I could go to the grocery store and buy a loaf of bread for $2.50. My dad used to tell me, "James, in the 1970s, five dollars could buy you steak, chicken, tons of bread, and all kinds of other things." I would often think, "Yeah, whatever, you're exaggerating." But when you look at the inflationary mechanisms deployed since the 1970s, you realize my dad wasn't exaggerating at all. To the contrary, he was understating it!

Consider the inflation we've seen in just the last few years. If you put $100,000 in the bank in 2020 and did nothing with it, that money now has the buying power of roughly $60,000.

We're watching inflation skyrocket. But when inflation spirals out of control, especially under a totalitarian ruler and during war, there's always a ruling class that is preserved.

"see thou hurt not the oil and the wine."

Revelation 6:6

Let's talk about what a loaf of bread will cost when the rider of the red horse appears. A single loaf will run anywhere from $150 to $500. Think about that for a second. It's going to be anywhere from one to three days' wages just for one loaf of bread.

When verse six says "not touching the oil and the wine," it means there will be a ruling class that will benefit from the war and chaos. You've heard of people like Soros, right? The wicked players tied to the World Economic Forum? The Clintons? These people grow wealthier during crises, often because of the crises themselves.

When a totalitarian ruler takes power, he ushers in war, then economic collapse. And during that collapse, the ruling class stays protected. That's exactly what will happen in the days of the final Antichrist.

The Pale Horse: Death Unleashed

"And when he had opened the fourth seal, I heard the voice of the fourth beast say, Come and see. And I looked, and behold a pale horse: and his name that sat on him was Death, and Hell followed with him. And power was given unto them over the fourth part of the earth, to kill with sword, and with hunger, and with death, and with the beasts of the earth."

Revelation 6:7–8

This is perhaps the most tragic part of this passage. I have to tell you, it's beyond sad. A quarter of the world's population doesn't die just from war. It's from the cascading fallout of everything that follows. War erupts, then economic collapse, followed by famine, and then plague. All these devastating consequences of war mean people will be dying left and right. It's heartbreaking.

That's the pattern. That's what it will look like when Christians are no longer in this world and the final Antichrist, no longer restrained, becomes a totalitarian ruler. Imagine how ugly that's going to be.

But here's something to be thankful for: God is using you as a preserving influence. How do Christians preserve? First, they're filled with the Spirit of God, which means they won't tolerate much of what they see happening around them. Second, they preserve when they speak up. They take a stand in the midst of wickedness.

We're watching history repeat itself. Right now, antisemitic sentiment has grown faster than it did in World War II Germany. It's far more extreme than it was even back then, and we should be alarmed.

Let me offer you something to take joy in, though: Christians can rejoice knowing we won't be here for what we just looked at in Revelation Chapter 6. Thank God! In the meantime, we have an obligation to be the preserving influence in this world. That means fight like we've never fought before. Fight the good fight. Do the work God has called you to do. Be aware. Open your eyes. Educate yourself in these things.

Beyond the Four Horsemen

We've read about all of this death and destruction, ending with the pale horse, and that's where we pick up with the fifth seal:

> "And when he had opened the fifth seal, I saw under the altar the souls of them that were slain for the Word of God, and for the testimony which they held: And they cried with a loud voice, saying, How long, O LORD, holy and true, dost thou not judge and avenge our blood on them that dwell on the earth? And white robes were given unto every one of them; and it was said unto them, that they should rest yet for a little season, until their fellowservants also and their brethren, that should be killed as they were,

should be fulfilled."

Revelation 6:9–11

I want to be clear about something important: these aren't Christians who were left behind. You need to understand that these aren't people who were left behind on earth after the church was raptured. These are people who chose to resist the Antichrist after the church was taken, and they were killed because of that resistance.

Let me point out a couple of things. First, most people living on earth at that time will be completely deceived. They'll actually believe that taking the mark of the beast is a righteous thing to do. It won't be easy to recognize evil and resist it. In fact, Revelation Chapter 14 tells us that people will be so convinced taking the mark of the beast is righteous that an angel will have to warn them: "Don't do this. If you do this, you will die." The warning will be crystal clear, and still, people will choose to ignore it.

Second, the martyrs who shed their blood during this time will come from a very small pool of people. It's foolish to think you can just miss the rapture and then somehow avoid the fallout of the war, the famine, the plagues, and still refuse to take the mark of the beast.

The impression we get from Revelation is that the world will see the Antichrist as the best thing since sliced bread. Most people will believe he's the answer to every problem. The Bible tells us that when he transforms into the beast in Revelation Chapter 13 and sets himself up in the temple, demanding to be worshiped, only a group of Jews will see him for who he really is. He'll heavily persecute and kill the

Jews, and then he'll kill everyone else who refuses to take the mark of the beast.

Keep this in mind: if you take the mark of the beast, you're done. You're doomed. There's no repentance. Take the mark, and you're going to hell. It's that simple.

I got myself in a little trouble when someone asked me about putting together a little package that Christians can leave behind for their loved ones. It would give instructions about what to do after the rapture happens, for those who are left here. I think the idea is actually pretty good. The problem is, if the rapture has already taken place and they've rejected God, they're not likely to listen to any message we leave behind. Why? Because they'll be so consumed by deception that they won't care what we have to say.

Many will think that what happened is actually a good thing. They may not even recognize what happened was the rapture as described in the Bible. They might actually look at it as some weird, crazy, hyper-humanistic, secular ejection of Mother Earth. Think that's crazy? Just listen to the speech King Charles gave at COP28. "We are going to be, those of us that fight the earth, are going to be rejected by the earth, because the earth is not here for us. We're here for the earth."

Man, the weirdness that comes out of these people's mouths is staggering.

Sadly, when all these signs and wonders happen and the world is pretty much in complete chaos, most people will continue to flip God off. They'll actually be more resolved in hating God as the world begins to fall apart.

We've all seen people with hard hearts. When things start

going really bad for them, what do they do? They get angrier and blame God.

The Sixth Seal: Cosmic Chaos

Look what it goes on to say in verses 12–17:

"And I beheld when he had opened the sixth seal, and, lo, there was a great earthquake; and the sun became black as sackcloth of hair, and the moon became as blood; And the stars of heaven fell unto the earth, even as a fig tree casteth her untimely figs, when she is shaken of a mighty wind. And the heaven departed as a scroll when it is rolled together; and every mountain and island were moved out of their places. And the kings of the earth, and the great men, and the rich men, and the chief captains, and the mighty men, and every bondman, and every free man, hid themselves in the dens and in the rocks of the mountains; And said to the mountains and rocks, Fall on us, and hide us from the face of Him that sitteth on the throne, and from the wrath of the Lamb: For the great day of his wrath is come; and who shall be able to stand?"

Revelation 6:12–17

It's fascinating how the Bible uses the image of a fig tree casting untimely figs.

My wife and I had a fig tree in the yard at our first house. One day a strong wind blew causing all the figs to fall prematurely. We had about fifty of them scattered across the yard. A few days later, they ripened in the grass. Our dog had a blast eating them all, but we were left disappointed.

When figs are almost ripe and ready to harvest, their connection to the tree weakens. They all reach this point at the same time, so even a gentle shake will make them fall.

This image of figs suddenly dropping from the tree prematurely is a stunning illustration of what's coming. The meteor shower the Bible describes here isn't what we typically picture; a few dozen streaks per hour or a brief flash across the night sky. Instead, meteors will fall from the sky like nothing anyone has ever witnessed. The sky will light up completely from the flames of these meteors falling to earth, like a fig tree shedding all its figs at once. It's almost unimaginable. A rocket blazing through the atmosphere is nothing compared to a massive meteor shower with hundreds falling to the ground every second. God's judgment will be terrifying and catastrophic.

> "And the heaven departed as a scroll when it is rolled together; and every mountain and island were moved out of their places."
>
> **Revelation 6:14**

I don't even want to imagine what it will look like when the heavens roll up like a scroll and every mountain and island is shaken from its place. No one wants to be here for that. At least those of us who have been raptured won't have to experience it.

The Universal Recognition

Think about this: how many people right now are shaking their fist at God? How many people are angry at Him? I've never understood this about atheists. Most are angry at someone they claim doesn't even exist. If God doesn't exist, how can they be angry at Him? Imagine an adult waking up in the morning and saying, "I'm just really, really angry at Santa Claus right now." It makes no sense.

What happens after that is even more alarming and heartbreaking. God is going to destroy the world, and when His judgment comes, people who have rejected Him their entire lives are going to speak to inanimate objects (mountains and caves) and beg them to fall on them to avoid the judgment God is bringing. They're going to look at the sky, and what they see will be so overwhelming that they'll run into a cave and hope it collapses on them. What's astounding is that the Bible makes it clear: all of the people experiencing this, watching the world fall apart around them, will know it's God judging them.

I don't care how hard your heart is or how much you continue to say that God doesn't exist. The question isn't whether you're going to believe in Him when that day comes. That's not the question. You will see it, and you will believe. Honestly, you may believe it now, but your heart is so hard and your seared conscience has kept you from accepting it. The real question is this: are you going to proclaim that He's real now and live according to His purpose, or are you going to discover that later and suffer an eternity in hell?

Getting With the Program

I know a couple of police officers (very sharp detectives). When they pick up violent gang members who try to resist arrest, they tell them, "Look, here's the deal. You can either choose to go with the program or we're going to force you to go with the program. But either way, you're going with the program." The reality is, they're going to jail. They're going to stand before the judge. They're going to have a trial with a jury if they choose to plead not guilty. But one way or another, they're going to go with the program, whether they like it or not.

Each of us is going to go with God's program. The question is: are you going to accept it now and experience every wonderful thing God has for you in the future, into eternity? Or are you going to reject it and regret it in hell for the rest of eternity?

If you're a Christian, there's another valid question for you. Will you resist God until the very end, barely making it into heaven by the skin of your teeth, having lived a miserable life because you resisted God? Or will you choose to say, "God, I'm going to listen to You, I'm going to do what You want me to do, and I'm going to experience life to the fullest, as You've called me to experience it"?

I can attest from personal experience: as a father, husband, and pastor, the life God has given me has its share of trials. Yes, there have been difficulties and hardships, but the life God has blessed me with has also been wonderful. It's not one I could have ever created for myself. God has given me this life, and I'm eternally grateful.

God is faithful. If we're willing to trust Him and seek Him, we'll not only avoid the judgment we're reading about in Revelation Chapter 6, but we'll experience the blessing that comes from knowing Him. We can do the work He's purposed for us and follow His plan, so we can live life to the fullest. That's the goal. These last days should be the most enjoyable days of our lives. The reality is, if you seek God and go with His program, you'll be the beneficiary of every wonderful thing He has for you.

The Four Horsemen of the Apocalypse represent a pattern we've seen throughout human history, but when they come riding in their final form, after the church has been removed, the devastation will be unlike anything the world has ever seen. Yet even in the midst of John's description of such terrible judgment, we find hope. We who trust in Christ will not be here to witness these horrors, and hope that God's ultimate plan is not destruction, but redemption).

As you watch the signs of the times we now live in and see the stage being set for these final events, be encouraged. Our redemption draws near, and Christ is coming soon.

The 144,000 and the Multitude

Before we dive into Revelation Chapter 7, I want to lay some groundwork about the importance of language. My parents were born and raised in Egypt, so Arabic was one of the languages spoken in our home. I've always been fascinated by linguistics: the study of languages, their structure, meaning, history, and how people use them. When people gather and speak in their native or shared language, that language doesn't just communicate words, it carries a cultural formation. It reflects the norms, experiences, and assumptions of the society or subgroup using it.

Take English, for example. There isn't just one "English"; there are countless dialects and subcultures within it. The same phrase can mean entirely different things depending on who's speaking and where they're from.

Let's say I'm in a room full of building inspectors. If I ask, "What's cracking?" One of them might respond with something like, "Not sure, could be a lateral fissure extending six inches from the pipe joint near the rafter." In their world, "cracking" has a very specific, technical meaning. But head to certain parts of Los Angeles or Southern California, and "What's cracking?" becomes a casual, friendly greeting like "What's up?" Same words, completely different meanings, all shaped by the culture and context they're spoken in.

Language changes and varies across every context. When used in a specific way, it carries distinct connotations. I want to say this right off the bat, I'm proud to be an American citizen. I love the English language. I think English is wonderful, and I spend considerable time learning how to wordsmith so I can communicate as effectively as possible in my videos, sermons, and writing.

However, there are major differences between English and Hebrew, and more importantly, between the cultures those languages represent. For students of the Bible, English often works against them. The way English functions, both grammatically and structurally, tends to dominate other languages in scriptural study. It sometimes overpowers the text's actual meaning, imposing connotations that differ significantly from the original.

Let me give you a modern-day example. Say I approach an English-speaking person in the United States and say, "I have a poem for you," then recite a piece of literature without any rhyme, or one that doesn't match what you and I think of as poetry. That person would look at me and say, "You're crazy. That's not a poem." For most Americans, a poem rhymes, like "Jack and Jill went up the hill," or "Humpty Dumpty sat on a wall, Humpty Dumpty had a great fall." But in most other languages, rhyme and similar phrase length aren't part of the poetic structure. In Japanese, for instance, haiku is a poetic form with three unrhymed lines following a 5-7-5 syllable structure, typically focusing on nature and a specific moment in time.

In Hebrew, poetry carries a completely different meaning from English. Greek also becomes significant when we look at the Book of Revelation, but I'm focusing on Hebrew because we're talking about the Old Testament, and Hebrew was the language it was mostly written in, with the exception of specific chapters written in Aramaic.

If you want to understand the Book of Revelation, you need to understand the Old Testament. To really understand the Old Testament, you need to understand Hebrew language and culture. I'm not saying you must be able to recite the Hebrew alphabet or perfectly pronounce Hebrew words. But you should understand the mindset and culture that shaped the language. Without understanding the culture behind the language, you'll miss the deeper meaning of what's being communicated.

Everything I just mentioned presents a series of problems that are often difficult to overcome without proper context. But when it comes to good Bible translation, there are other variables we must consider as they relate to functional linguistics.

Another significant issue is, the Hebrew language represented in the Bible is technically a dead language. Biblical Hebrew is still studied, read, and used in liturgy today, but it's considered "dead" in the sense that it is no longer a naturally evolving spoken language. It functions as a historically fixed form of Hebrew.

Modern Hebrew helps us understand many concepts in

biblical Hebrew, but some ideas and cultural nuances run much deeper. Hebrew, like many Semitic languages, requires you to approach translation using a principle called *dynamic equivalence*, meaning a thought-for-thought approach rather than word-for-word. This method demands a clear understanding of context, which means understanding cultural elements that may feel foreign to us today, given how far removed we are from the historical setting.

Here's an example of how rapidly language and culture can shift. Try reading an original 1611 King James Bible in its Elizabethan English form. Most people today would struggle to read it because the language has changed so dramatically. Some of that change stems from evolving language structure and grammatical rules, but much of it comes from shifting cultural contexts.

Translation is a complicated endeavor. I encourage you to dive deeper into that subject, but for now, I'll give you a high-level overview to give you a solid foundation for understanding the message in its fullness.

Hebrew Storytelling vs. Western Narrative

In America and across most Western cultures, we tell stories by starting at the beginning and moving straight through to the end. Very linear, without jumping around. This is especially true in court. An experienced attorney will tell you, "Don't be all over the place. Stick to a timeline and walk me through it from start to finish." Witnesses are instructed not to insert their opinions or internal thoughts anywhere in that timeline, because doing so might confuse the jury. Confuse a jury, and you create reasonable doubt.

But language doesn't necessarily drive culture. More often, it's the other way around: culture dictates language. With that in mind, you'll see that Hebrew storytelling works completely differently.

Hebrew storytelling, like that found in African, Middle Eastern, and some Asian cultures, doesn't unfold chronologically. Instead, stories center on a specific moment or idea, then build outward by layering in key details around that central point. A Hebrew storyteller sees the whole arc of what happened, then shares observations about different moments or the central figure.

Here's an example: "James is a loving father who does anything for his children. He stayed up several nights when his little one was sick. Oh, and he prays over them every night, just as he has since they were infants. Oh, and he once sat with his daughter and told her she's the apple of God's eye. Oh, and he trains them in the ways of the LORD. This is why I know James adores his children." The more information the storyteller shares, the more "Oh, by the way's", the clearer the picture becomes. The ancient biblical audience understood this instinctively.

Here's an example from the Bible. Genesis 1:1 says, "In the beginning God created the heavens and the earth." Then verse two says, "And the earth was without form and void." Some people believe something happened between these two verses. They see a chronological gap and call it the *gap theory*. Many American preachers argue that when God created the heavens and the earth, He created them perfectly. But since verse two describes the earth as without form and void, they conclude something must have gone wrong to leave it in that state.

I want to pause here for just a moment to show you how shallow this interpretation really is, even in their perception of what they consider perfect. This reflects Western thinking, where perfection, to an overwhelming majority of minds, centers on the idea that everything must arrive as a finished product. That expectation is a construct of our culture's own definition of perfection.

In a God-centered culture, the understanding of perfection is framed within the process of creation itself; the beauty found in the journey of forming and fashioning. What we're seeing here, as you'll soon discover, is a description of God creating the raw materials He would later shape into something extraordinary. That reality is difficult for many to grasp.

One of the best ways to illustrate this is through the real estate market in the United States. Most people won't even consider buying a home that's still under construction because they can't visualize its completion. They want something turnkey, something polished and ready to move into. That mindset mirrors the same cultural bias driving the flawed conclusion I'm about to explain.

Hebrew culture approaches the Creation account from a completely different perspective. In Hebrew thought, the author begins with a declaration: "God created the heavens and the earth. I want everyone to know, "Hey, that guy over there, God, He's the one who created everything." Then the author circles back to an earlier moment: "Now let me tell you how it happened. God created the raw material. The earth was formless and empty. He started with this raw material, then began shaping and molding it."

Most people don't realize that the Book of Genesis, originally written in biblical Hebrew, doesn't tell the story of God's creation chronologically. Genesis Chapter 1 presents a structured, six-day account of how the universe and life came to be. The second account then zooms in to provide richer detail about God's creation of the Garden of Eden, Adam and Eve, and their story.

The Hebrew Pattern in Revelation

Now let's look at Revelation Chapter 7, where things become much clearer. In Revelation Chapter 6, we covered the first six seals. What happens in Revelation Chapter 7 takes place while the first six seals are unfolding. And remember, those first six seals cover events throughout the entire tribulation period. You saw the White Horse Rider introduced, the Antichrist, but you won't read about his totalitarian rule until Revelation Chapter 13.

Revelation Chapter 7 describes a group of people living during the tribulation. This isn't referring to Christians who have already been raptured. In fact, the next time we see the saints, us Christians who have been raptured, is in Revelation Chapter 20. It's crucial that you understand this. Once you do, you won't make the same mistakes others have made when interpreting the timelines in the Book of Revelation.

The Four Angels and the Winds

"And after these things I saw four angels standing on the four corners of the earth, holding the four winds of the earth, that the wind should not blow on the earth, nor on the sea, nor on any tree."

Revelation 7:1

The wind stopping is kind of a crazy picture. I can't imagine what it would look like if the wind stopped in Los Angeles alone. Picture the smoggy air just settling over the city. It would create a terrible mess. Thank God there's at least a little breeze blowing through LA every day, pushing out all that nasty air. To have no wind anywhere? Absolutely devastating.

In recent years, some people have surprisingly theorized that the earth is flat. We know that nothing could be further from the truth. The Bible confirms that the earth is round.

However, for the sake of argument, let's examine one of the main biblical passages Flat Earthers use to "prove" the earth is flat: Revelation 7:1, which mentions the four corners of the earth. What the Apostle John was actually referring to is north, south, east, and west.

Not only did Pythagoras and Aristotle prove the earth is a sphere as early as the fourth century, but the Bible had made it very clear long before anyone even thought about it. The oldest book in the Bible, presumably the Book of Job, tells us about the circle of the earth. Other passages talk about it being dark in one place while it's light in another, further confirming the earth's spherical shape.

We still use this figurative language today. When we talk about searching for people around the world, we use the colloquialism, "We searched the four corners of the earth." Even the United States Marine Corps uses the phrase, "We've gone to all four quarters of the world," as a long-standing metaphor for the four cardinal directions: north, south, east, and west.

Notice that God didn't say He would remove your sins as far as north is from south. If you started traveling from the North Pole, you'd eventually reach a definitive point when you arrived at the South Pole. But Psalm 103:12 states, "As far as the east is from the west, so far hath He removed our transgressions from us." God's Word uses the infinite distance between east and west to illustrate how completely He removes transgressions from believers. Our sins aren't just covered or partially removed, they're completely separated to a point that's unreachable. God already knew what the early Greek philosophers and Magellan wouldn't discover until the 15th century!

The Sealing of the 144,000

"And I saw another angel ascending from the east, having the seal of the living God: and He cried with a loud voice to the four angels, to whom it was given to hurt the earth and the sea, Saying, Hurt not the earth, neither the sea, nor the trees, till we have sealed the servants of our God in their foreheads. And I heard the number of them which were sealed: and there were sealed an hundred and forty and four thousand of all the tribes of the children of Israel."

Revelation 7:2–4

I'm asked all the time about the seal on the angel ascending from the east and the seal that will be placed on the 144,000. Some people think it's a number. Others believe it's some sort of physical mark. Still others imagine it's like a halo floating above the angel. I don't know what it is. The Bible doesn't tell us. What I do know is that it's something used to identify these people. Not necessarily by the rest of the world, but by the four angels who were given power to hurt the earth and the sea. Here's what's remarkable: the people who have been sealed before the wind stops, before the asteroids fall, before the other calamities come. They will be completely unaffected.

I don't know what the seal is, but I do know who receives it. That's an easy one! First of all, they're not Jehovah's Witnesses. If you want to turn a Jehovah's Witness's world upside down, just point out that their religion states none of them should be here today. When they began in the late 1870s, there were only a few hundred of them. They believed that when they reached 144,000 followers, they'd be taken up to heaven. The problem is, according to their own stats, there are about 8.8 million followers today. That means 98.4% are headed to hell by their own account. We don't have to question who the 144,000 in the Bible are. We know.

The 144,000 are Jews, literal descendants of Abraham, Isaac, and Jacob.

Contrary to growing popular belief, the church isn't spiritual Israel. It's a distinct body of believers, separate from God's ancestrally chosen people. Throughout the Bible, God repeatedly reaffirms His promise to Israel, and that promise extends into the very time we're reading about now.

Scripture shows us again and again that God's promises to His people are irrevocable. In Genesis 17:7, for example, the LORD declares, "And I will establish my covenant between me and thee and thy seed after thee in their generations for an everlasting covenant, to be a God unto thee, and to thy seed after thee."

Jeremiah 31:35–37 declares, "Thus saith the LORD, which giveth the sun for a light by day, and the ordinances of the moon and of the stars for a light by night, which divideth the sea when the waves thereof roar; The LORD of hosts is His name: If those ordinances depart from before me, saith the LORD, then the seed of Israel also shall cease from being a nation before me for ever. Thus saith the LORD; If heaven above can be measured, and the foundations of the earth searched out beneath, I will also cast off all the seed of Israel for all that they have done, saith the LORD."

Leviticus 26:44 further confirms this, saying, "And yet for all that, when they be in the land of their enemies, I will not cast them away, neither will I abhor them, to destroy them utterly, and to break my covenant with them: for I am the LORD their God." Isaiah 14:1 adds, "For the LORD will have mercy on Jacob, and will yet choose Israel, and set them in their own land: and the strangers shall be joined with them, and they shall cleave to the house of Jacob."

If you doubt my assertion based on what I've quoted from the Old Testament, perhaps the most definitive confirmation comes from the Book of Romans, where the Apostle Paul writes, "For the gifts and calling of God are without repentance" (Romans 11:29). In context, Paul is speaking about Israel. God is declaring that His promise to Israel is irrevocable.

So let me reiterate: we're talking about real Jews. These will be Jews who very likely come to a saving knowledge of

God after the rapture, during the tribulation. They'll see what's happening, recognize it as the hand of God, repent, and put their faith in Jesus. And here's something remarkable: they will become the greatest evangelists who have ever walked the earth. They will be the most powerful preachers delivering the most compelling message!

I believe this is already true of today's Jewish brothers and sisters who come to Christ. I have many Jewish friends who don't know the LORD yet, and I tell them, "If you come to know Jesus, you will be the most astounding representative of the LORD."

My Jewish friend, David Tal, is a tank commander, a major in the Israeli Defense Force. He speaks multiple languages, understands different cultures, and has extensive experience on the military field and in diplomatic units representing Israel. David is a brilliant guy. He often guides groups and individuals on tours of the Holy Land and has spoken with some of the most respected preachers in the world. In his genuine search to understand, he would ask questions about Christianity. David asks hard questions, and these people would often get offended and respond, "You're just trying to shut me up, you hard-hearted Jew."

David would come to me with the hard questions, and we'd get into aggressive, drag-out, Middle Eastern–style debates, just yelling at each other, because that's what we do in Middle Eastern culture. He and I would go back and forth, sometimes mixing in Hebrew and Arabic words. One time at a hamburger stand near my church, our debate got so heated that I shouted, "You're not going to hell. I'm not going to let you go to hell. You're going to get saved! One day, you wait and see!"

As you might have guessed, God got hold of David's heart several years later. The story of how David got saved is pretty amazing. Here's a guy who lives in a town in Israel, in the middle of everything, and he comes all the way to Seal Beach, California, where he gives his life to Christ on the pier, not in the middle of Jerusalem. God's sense of humor is incredible.

I used to tell David, "When God gets ahold of you, you're going to be so much more powerful, bro. You have no idea." And it's been greater than I ever imagined. Because of his deep knowledge of Christ and his passion for glorifying God, thousands of people now follow him online. They're blown away by his immense knowledge and understanding of things American culture doesn't understand. David's background, his geographical and biblical cultural awareness, makes him an incredible witness and preacher of the Gospel. When you read about the 144,000 in Revelation Chapter 7, remember these are Jews. And I'm telling you right now, they're going to be the best evangelists in the world.

I wear a set of Israeli dog tags inscribed with "Bring them home" in English and "Our heart is in Gaza" in Hebrew. I won't take them off until every Israeli hostage is accounted for and brought home.

While the Bring Them Home movement in Israel is primarily directed against Prime Minister Benjamin Netanyahu, I want to be clear: when I wear these dog tags or the ribbon, I don't stand with that movement. For the record, I believe Benjamin Netanyahu will go down as one of Israel's greatest prime ministers, and that God has undoubtedly placed him in Israel for such a time as this.

One of the reasons I wear these items is to stand in solidarity with the Jewish people, a commitment I made gladly when they were given to me by an October 7 survivor and former hostage. I promised I would never stop wearing them until the remains of the last hostages are returned.

Why? Because God used the Jewish people to preserve the Bible for us, even when some I've met in Israel have turned away from Him. We should love and cherish the Jews. They are not simply a national treasure; they are a world treasure.

These 144,000 Jews are going to be powerful communicators of the Gospel.

The Tribes Listed

Which Jews are we talking about? This is where it gets interesting. The Bible makes it very clear. Before we dive in, I need to mention something important: you can't verify tribal lineage today. When Titus destroyed the temple in 70 AD, the genealogical records were destroyed along with it. Everything after that was passed down verbally. So it's nearly impossible to establish lineage the way the Bible originally prescribed. But here's the thing: God knows. He doesn't need those records to know who's from the tribe of Naphtali or Gad or any of the others.

Now look at this, it's fascinating. God gets specific here, because a lot of people claim, "We are these Hebrew Israelites." If you've heard about the Black Hebrew Israelite movement, they build entire arguments on the lost tribes of Israel. But here's the truth: God hasn't lost any tribes. He tells us exactly who these tribes are. He's not beating around the bush.

Revelation 7:5–8 states:

"Of the tribe of Judah were sealed twelve thousand."

"Of the tribe of Reuben were sealed twelve thousand."

"Of the tribe of Gad were sealed twelve thousand."

"Of the tribe of Aser were sealed twelve thousand."

"Of the tribe of Nepthalim were sealed twelve thousand."

"Of the tribe of Manasses were sealed twelve thousand."

"Of the tribe of Simeon were sealed twelve thousand."

"Of the tribe of Levi were sealed twelve thousand."

"Of the tribe of Issachar were sealed twelve thousand."

"Of the tribe of Zabulon were sealed twelve thousand."

"Of the tribe of Joseph were sealed twelve thousand."

"Of the tribe of Benjamin were sealed twelve thousand."

That's the complete list God gives us. Now, I want to point out a couple of interesting details here.

First, if the Bible only mentioned Joseph's tribe without naming either of his sons, you might assume it's using a general term. But that doesn't quite add up, because one of Joseph's sons is actually included in this list.

Here's the other thing: The tribe of Levi appears in this list, though it's usually absent from previous ones. But the tribe of Dan is missing. So Levi's in, Dan's out. And what other tribe is absent? Ephraim. Remember Joseph's two sons, Ephraim and Manasseh? Ephraim isn't mentioned, only Manasseh. This is really strange.

Now, let's look at some historical context. First, it wasn't unusual for tribal lists to exclude certain tribes. For example, you rarely, if ever, see Joseph listed as a tribe of Israel. Instead, you see his sons Ephraim and Manasseh, often called the "half-tribe of Ephraim" and the "half-tribe of Manasseh." It's also common for Levi to be left out of tribal lists. Why? Most lists were connected to land allocations, especially in the Book of Joshua. When land was distributed, God made it clear that the tribe of Levi would receive no territory. Their portion was him alone.

So, the idea is you'd never see Levi mentioned because the lists were typically tied to land inheritance. Does that mean Levi wasn't a tribe? Of course not. Levi was absolutely a tribe. It just wasn't mentioned because it didn't need to be. It makes sense that Levi appears in Revelation, since you'd expect the Levites to be some of the most powerful witnesses of the Gospel, being the priestly tribe.

But why don't we see Ephraim mentioned here? And what about Dan? These are valid questions, important ones, actually. And while we're at it, why would Joseph be mentioned at all?

I think "Joseph" serves as a broad term here. When the text refers to the tribe of Joseph, it likely encompasses all of Joseph's descendants, not just Ephraim's line, but other descendants who remain connected to the Jewish order as well.

But perhaps more significantly, when we ask why Dan and Ephraim aren't mentioned, we're asking a tough but fair question. Let me be straight with you. As someone who's spent over thirty years studying the Bible, my honest answer is: I don't know. And I don't think anyone should claim to know, because God never told us why. I'll tell you this, though: when I sought an answer many years ago, one major thing stood out: something both Dan and Ephraim had in common, and this is crucial.

Dan and Ephraim were the first two tribes to embrace idolatry. Could that be why God doesn't mention them here? I don't know. Remember, if you're a tribe of Israel and you're not on this list, it doesn't mean you don't exist, or that you're worthless, or that you're out of the picture. It simply means you're not among those who will be protected during this time. That's all it means. Could it be related to idolatry? I'm not sure why.

Keeping this in mind, and at the risk of sounding redundant, I really don't know why this is happening. But I want to offer some thoughts that might help us apply this to how we live. There are a couple of theological points worth considering here.

One of the most important is that we often become like what we worship. We assimilate into the very thing we bow down to, and that's a scary thought if what we worship is anything other than the true and living God. Here's something worth noting: if you pursue idolatry, you'd be foolish to think you can also seek protection from the true and living God. If you choose to worship a false god, I believe God will let you do so, but He'll also let you face the world around you without His protection.

Could this be why we don't see these tribes mentioned?

I'm not going to say definitively that this is the reason, but I will tell you this should be a powerful moment in our reading of Revelation. It reminds us that if we want God's protection, we must do things God's way. We must worship Him on His terms.

The Great Multitude from the Tribulation

"After this I beheld, and, lo, a great multitude, which no man could number, of all nations, and kindreds, and people, and tongues, stood before the throne, and before the Lamb, clothed with white robes, and palms in their hands."

Revelation 7:9

Here we have a remarkable opportunity to draw another parallel from the Old Testament, one that's consequential to understanding what we're actually seeing in Revelation.

First, we need to talk about the Feast of Tabernacles (Sukkot). Let's focus on Leviticus 23:40, which says, "And ye shall take you on the first day the boughs of goodly trees, branches of palm trees, and the boughs of thick trees, and willows of the brook; and ye shall rejoice before the LORD your God seven days." During Sukkot, Israel would wave palm branches as a sign of victory and as an expression of joy in celebrating God's presence with them.

It was very important because the older generation used it to teach the younger generation about God's provision, protection, and deliverance from the difficulties the Israelites faced as they traveled through the wilderness.

In Revelation Chapter 7, we see something remarkable:

a great multitude rejoicing before the throne because their proverbial wilderness journey on earth is over. They're celebrating God's deliverance and the fact that His presence is now with them forever.

If you think about it, this scene is essentially the final fulfillment of Sukkot, God tabernacling with His people. I should note here that we'll see this referenced again in Revelation 21:3: "And I heard a great voice out of heaven saying, Behold, the tabernacle of God is with men, and He will dwell with them, and they shall be His people, and God Himself shall be with them, and be their God."

This beautiful picture offers us hope in ways many of us never imagined. Having a relationship with God that extends into eternity is something we never thought possible, but God made it possible through what He did for us.

Many people read verse nine and assume it describes the church, but it doesn't. How do we know? Because John the Apostle has no idea who these people are. If he knew, he would have told us. But he didn't. This isn't the church. These are people who died during the tribulation and refused to take the mark of the beast. These are the same people I mentioned back in Chapter 6, the ones I said we'd eventually discuss here in Chapter 7.

> "And cried with a loud voice, saying, Salvation to our God which sitteth upon the throne, and unto the Lamb. And all the angels stood round about the throne, and about the elders and the four beasts, and fell before the throne on their faces, and worshiped God, Saying, Amen: Blessing, and glory, and wisdom, and thanks-

giving, and honour, and power, and might, be unto our God for ever and ever. Amen. And one of the elders answered, saying unto me, What are these which are arrayed in white robes? and whence came they?"

Revelation 7:10–13

Who are these people? Where did they come from? Look at John's answer. He didn't say, "Oh, it's the church, it's us." Here's what he actually said:

"And I said unto him, Sir, thou knowest. And He said to me, These are they which came out of great tribulation, and have washed their robes, and made them white in the blood of the Lamb."

Revelation 7:14

There's your answer. He's telling us plainly: these are people who came out of the great tribulation, who washed their robes and made them white in the blood of the Lamb.

"Therefore are they before the throne of God, and serve Him day and night in His temple: and He that sitteth on the throne shall dwell among them."

Revelation 7:15

By the way, Revelation Chapter 20 marks the first time the church is mentioned again. And by then, we're in an entirely different place.

The Reality Check

Look at this, because it's critical. So many people cling to this idea and say, "Well, I'm going to live how I want right now." Someone recently told me, "I believe everything you're saying, James. When you're raptured and I'm left behind, I'll just refuse the mark."

My response is always the same: if you won't do something as simple as saying, "Christ, please come into my life. I put my faith and trust in You," because you'd rather party at the clubs, live with someone you're dating, or keep doing things you know go against God's will for your life, then there's no way you'll refuse the mark of the beast later. If you won't stand for Jesus now, you won't stand for Him then.

It's like what I tell single women when they talk about their non-Christian, work-in-progress boyfriend: "Oh, he's going to be such a wonderful man to marry." No, he's not going to be wonderful. He's going to be terrible. Run! He's got a potty mouth, an anger problem, he pressures you sexually, and he doesn't respect your boundaries. But you think, "When we get married, he'll change. We'll read devotions together." The truth? When you get married, he'll be worse.

My point is: if you're sitting here right now saying you'd never accept the mark of the beast, that's baloney. You're making that claim in the most ideal circumstances imaginable. When it actually comes down to a life-or-death decision to take the mark or reject it, what will you do? Yeah, you'll take it. I don't mean to be harsh, but let's be real. During COVID, we watched millions of Americans face a choice: get an experimental and unproven jab or lose your job. If millions couldn't stand up for that, how will they stand up when the government says, "No mark, no food"? I don't see most people refusing it when their survival is on the line.

Please hear my heart: if you received the jab, there's no condemnation here. I'm not judging anyone. What I'm pointing out is the totalitarianism that came with that whole situation. The bottom line is this: if you haven't already, please receive Christ now so you don't have to face the decision of whether to take the mark.

Do it now. What you do today will echo through eternity. I'm not asking you to stop going to the club or give up everything you enjoy. God will work on those things in His own time. Just put your faith and trust in Christ Jesus. Let God change you from the inside out. Let Him transform you. Then watch what happens.

The Promise of Comfort

Look what it goes on to say, and I love this:

"They shall hunger no more, neither thirst any more; neither shall the sun light on them, nor any heat. For the Lamb which is in the midst of the throne shall feed them, and shall lead them unto living fountains of waters: and God shall wipe away all tears from their eyes."

Revelation 7:16–17

Isn't that powerful? People often ask me, "When it says God will wipe away our tears, does that mean we won't experience any sorrow in heaven?" I don't have the full answer to that. When the Bible tells us God will wipe away our tears, what exactly is He wiping away? Are they tears of sadness over what we've witnessed: the knowledge that some of our loved ones aren't with us? Or are they tears of overwhelming joy in that moment? I don't know. But here's what I do know: what we have waiting for us in eternity is incredible. And what awaits this earth? Not so much. There's tremendous power in knowing the LORD right here, right now, in this very moment. And by the way, it's a better life too, I promise!

Let me leave you with this: if you're a believer, this world is the closest you'll ever come to hell. If you're not a believer, savor this world while you can. It's the closest you'll ever come to heaven. My hope is that every person recognizes where we are in this day and this moment, and that everyone would love the LORD and serve Him with their whole heart and life.

As we continue unpacking this story, you're going to be amazed as we move closer to the time when the Antichrist comes into full power. It's going to blow your mind, but you'll also be encouraged by what we read. It will strengthen and encourage you, because all the crazy things you're seeing in the world today will start to make sense. You'll understand, because the Bible already told us it was coming!

The 144,000 represent God's faithfulness to preserve a remnant even in the darkest hour. They are His sealed witnesses who will proclaim the Gospel with power unlike anything the world has ever seen. And the great multitude from every nation? They remind us that even in the midst of unprecedented tribulation, God's grace will still reach hearts around the globe.

As we see the stage being set for these final events, let's be encouraged that God is sovereign, His plans are perfect, and His people, whether raptured before or saved during the tribulation, will ultimately be with Him forever.

Silence in Heaven

God functions in a predictable way in one sense (and I use that terminology carefully). I say "in one sense" because while God is infinite and beyond full human comprehension, He's also perfectly consistent in His nature and actions, which makes His patterns predictable to the extent that we, in our limited capacity, can discern them. The seeming unpredictability of God isn't a reflection of instability or contradiction but rather a product of our inability to perceive His thoughts in their fullness.

> As the Bible says, "For my thoughts are not your thoughts, neither are your ways my ways, saith the LORD."
>
> **Isaiah 55:8**

What He says is true, and what He says He will do, He always accomplishes. He graciously gives us insight before executing judgment because He wants us to understand His heart and His ways.

When it comes to discernible patterns of judgment, how

we should live our lives, and the general heartbeat and ebb and flow of the Bible, you can see it clearly when you study the Word of God. You'll see the parallels, how they exist and reinforce each other throughout Scripture.

Understanding God's Judgment Pattern

You also need to understand that when God judges, His judgment is tied to how people exercise their free will in ways that go against what He says He wants for us and for any nation. The idea is this: when God begins to judge a nation or a people group, He starts by giving them exactly what they want.

Let me give you an example. What we're seeing in the United States right now is indeed the judgment of God. And when you look at someone like Joe Biden, the former president, understand this: Joe Biden was a function of God's judgment on this country.

Why? Because America had an insatiable appetite, literally an unquenchable hunger for sin. It had an appetite to pursue ungodliness. And God said, "Okay, if you want sin, if you want ungodliness, you can have it." So when people are allowed to run with that desire, you get leaders like Biden, who wasn't running a presidential administration but a totalitarian regime.

Under his regime, abortion skyrocketed. We witnessed countless other troubling changes unfold under his leadership. The wickedness of drag queens in libraries, the sexual exploitation of children disguised as health education in schools, all of this material being pushed on kids as young as kindergarten. It's all a function of God's judgment. It's God saying, "Here you go, mankind. You can have what you want."

But it's the believers who should be held accountable for what we saw. When they choose not to take a stand on these issues, this is the result.

When spiritual leaders absolve themselves from the political issues of the day, they invite God's judgment. They're allowing it in. They're the literal agents of that judgment. Because when you see wickedness all around you and say, "I'm going to stay silent," you create the very problems you're witnessing.

So much of God's judgment centers around Him saying, "You want it? You can have it." You don't have to read the Book of Revelation to understand what's coming. We see this pattern throughout Scripture. In Exodus, even as early as Genesis. When man has an insatiable appetite for lust and wickedness, God says, "I'm going to judge you by letting you have what you want."

A powerful example of this appears in how God judged Pharaoh and the Egyptians. When you read through Exodus, you discover that the Egyptians actually worshiped frogs. They viewed them as sacred and wove them into their religious system.

So when God sent the plague of frogs upon Egypt in Exodus 8:1–6, He essentially gave them what they wanted. The frogs multiplied everywhere, covering their homes, their land, and even their food. It became unbearable, and Pharaoh begged Moses to ask God to remove the frogs (Exodus 8:8–9).

When God did, the frogs all died, and the Egyptians gathered them into heaps throughout the land (Exodus 8:13–14). Yet because they worshiped frogs, they refused to burn them. Those piles of rotting frogs became the perfect breeding ground for the flies that descended on Egypt in the next plague (Exodus 8:20–24).

Ironic, isn't it?. The very thing they worshiped became the source of their misery. This demonstrates how God's judgment operates according to the desires of those who refuse to turn from sin. In His justice, God allowed them to be consumed by the very thing they exalted above Him.

Looking at Revelation Chapter 6 and the seals described there, here's something crucial to understand: the first four seals represent God's judgment of mankind, but not in the way you might expect. God judges by allowing people to have exactly what they want.

So what are these first four seals? Totalitarian rulers. War. Economic failure and collapse. Then death. This same pattern exists within governments today. When a government operates in totalitarianism, it's the result of sin within that society.

The Structure of Revelation's Judgments

There's a fascinating pattern of judgments in the Book of Revelation: a trilogy of escalating judgments.

The seven seals are opened, (Revelation Chapters 6–8), followed by the seven trumpets (Revelation Chapters 8–11), and finally, seven bowls (Revelation Chapters 15–16). In this progressive series of judgments, each set introduces the next, with the seventh judgment of the previous one kicking off the next. The judgments build in intensity and affect larger portions of the earth and mankind.

As the judgments unfold, each set is interrupted by inter-

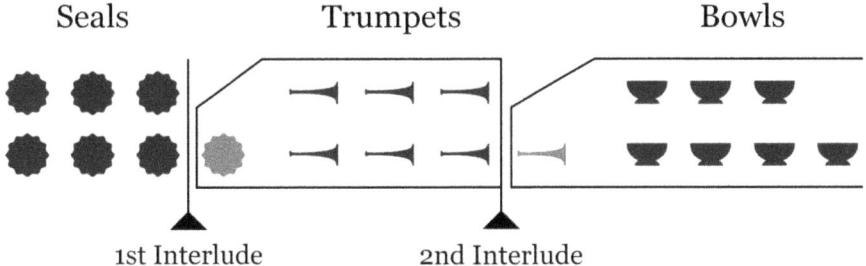

ludes where John sees visions of the sealed people of God and a heavenly battle taking place. These interludes don't disrupt the escalating sequence of the judgments themselves, but they do give us context.

When we pick up where we left off in Revelation Chapter 7, the first interlude has just taken place. Now we're moving into the seventh judgment seal, which introduces the trumpet judgments.

When the seventh seal opens, something extraordinary happens that opens the door into the next set of trumpet judgments. It all starts in Revelation 8:1.

The Seventh Seal: Silence in Heaven

"And when He had opened the seventh seal, there was silence in heaven about the space of half an hour."

Revelation 8:1

Thirty minutes of silence would be pretty awkward, right? If I just stared at you for ten seconds, you'd probably think, "What's happening? Is James having a meltdown?" We're so used to filling every quiet moment with distractions like music, texting, scrolling through social media. Think about stepping into an elevator with strangers and that super awkward silence while everyone waits to reach the lobby. The second those doors open, we bolt. Now imagine what it'll be like when the seventh seal is opened and there's silence in heaven for half an hour.

One of the qualities I inherited from my dad is his boldness and his default volume, which is often very loud. Around kids especially, I sometimes walk on eggshells because not everyone's used to a guy who operates at that volume. But my dad? He was always that way.

I'll never forget the time we lit firecrackers in my grandfather's church on New Year's Eve. I was in junior high, and my buddies, my brother, and I thought we had the perfect plan. Right before midnight, as the lights dimmed and the congregation began to pray, we snuck up to the baptismal, lit our firecrackers, and shouted "Happy New Year!" at the top of our lungs.

Most parents, knowing their kids were the culprits, would pretend it wasn't their children out of sheer embarrassment. After the initial shock of the loud fireworks popping in the baptismal, everyone kept praying. Not my dad. Without missing a beat, he and another father jumped up and chased my buddies and me backstage. As we ran for our lives, I could hear him yelling, "Come on, get back over here!" When they caught us, we got the spanking of a lifetime. That's just the way it was. Why? Because my dad cared about one thing: doing what was right in the eyes of God and raising his children well.

My dad taught me that the people in our lives, especially

our children and communities, need strong, godly, male leadership. But strong male leadership isn't just about being loud. Men need to live principled lives and speak up when it matters. True boldness isn't measured by the volume of your voice. It's the strength you carry, an uncompromising spirit, and a willingness to stand up for biblical principles. What I learned watching my dad shaped the man I am today.

When it came time for my dad to discipline us, we often felt the quiet before the storm. If you were raised with a loud dad, you know the moments that filled you with the fear of God were when dad went silent. My dad had a way of saying something in Arabic that we all understood, even though it sounded harmless to anyone else. He would say رح انت (inta ḥurr), which literally means "you're free." But in the Egyptian dialect, that phrase carries a very different meaning. It wasn't permission; it was a warning.

What he was really saying was, "Go ahead and do what you want, but you're going to face the consequences." And when my dad said it, we knew exactly what it meant. It meant, "You're free for now, because I'm going to go compose myself. But when I come back, all hell is going to break loose." That phrase has stuck with me for years because it perfectly captures how God often deals with rebellion. He allows people to choose their own way, even when that choice leads to destruction. It's as though He says, "You're free," but that freedom comes with the weight of judgment for what follows.

When my dad went silent like that, we'd immediately scramble to find chores to do. If we could've built him another house, we would have. That's how badly we knew consequences were coming. That was the generation I was raised in, and quite honestly, we need more of it today. Especially strong fathers.

The beautiful thing about my dad's silence was that he paused when he recognized his anger rising. He let it diminish. He cleared his mind, then chose how to respond. His loving discipline focused on one thing: getting rid of anything in us that would destroy what God had made good in our lives. When dad got quiet, it was scary, and the consequences that followed were never fun, but they were exactly what we needed.

The Noisiness of the World

We live in a world filled with noise. It's everywhere you turn, and I don't mean loud mouths like me, although there are plenty of those. I'm talking about an unrelenting noise that smothers our thoughts and clarity of mind. We experience it through our phones, in video games, and in the background music pumped into grocery stores, restaurants, gyms, and clubs. It's hard to escape this culture of noise.

Apple developed augmented reality goggles with built-in speakers that let users constantly see and hear digital content layered over the real world. Other companies are racing to build similar glasses and headsets you never have to remove, so that no matter what you're doing, you'll always have sounds and images overlaid on your physical surroundings. One of the dangers, however, is that we become addicted to constant noise and screen time. Much like someone fighting for sobriety from substance abuse or alcoholism, this addiction severely affects our discernment and ability to see things clearly.

This is why so many young people can't even look another person in the eyes when they talk to them. They've spent so much time engrossed in screens and noise that their awareness of others and attention span have completely vanished. They can't shake hands. They can't sit down and hold a conversation. They don't want to be around people. They have zero patience. Why? Because the digital world has robbed them of everything.

The Silence Before the Storm

And that's what's taking place here in Revelation. The noisiness of the world will grow louder than ever before. With Christians raptured, no one will remain to stand against the constant barrage of the world and its noisiness.

But at one point, God will declare, "Enough." When that seal breaks, every person on earth will experience thirty minutes of God's quiet before the storm. It will be a tremendously sobering silence, one that forces people to stop and think about the mistakes they've made. During that silence, mankind will think, What have we done? Silence. What have we gotten ourselves into?

By the way, it's healthy for believers to create moments of silence in our lives so we can make room for God to speak to us. I treasure days when I can shut everything down and rest in peace and quiet. I don't get many of those days, but I gain the most clarity in my mind and heart when I step away from all the noise.

The Seven Angels and the Incense

"And I saw the seven angels which stood before God,

and to them were given seven trumpets."

Revelation 8:2

Interesting to know, of the seven angels mentioned, two of them are Michael and Gabriel. The Apocrypha names the other five, but I don't know how credible that is.

"And another angel came and stood at the altar, having a golden censer; and there was given unto him much incense, that he should offer it with the prayers of all saints upon the golden altar which was before the throne. And the smoke of the incense, which came with the prayers of the saints, ascended up before God out of the angel's hand."

Revelation 8:3–4

I want to pause here, because many people read passages like this in Revelation and think, "Man, the guy writing about what he saw must have been on some kind of bad acid trip." They read these descriptions and are taken aback by how strange they seem. Let me point out two things right away.

First, imagine being John, living in that day, having never seen a watch, an airplane, or most things we experience in our modern world. If we hit the rewind button just thirty years, there are things we never could have imagined then. What's common for us today, email, smartphones, LED boards in stadiums, and streaming services, would have seemed unimaginable. As technology evolves, it creates new vocabulary: "flatscreen," "Siri," "smartwatch," and "social media."

When John describes certain things, he's using older terminology because he didn't have the words to describe the future. That's the first thing, he's describing future events using language from the past. But here's what I must emphasize: John doesn't spend most of his time doing that. He's mostly drawing on Old Testament concepts.

The Old Testament Foundation

When God told Moses to build the tabernacle, He gave him very specific instructions and detailed specifications. There was a good reason for this precision: based on what we read in the Old Testament, the tabernacle was more than just a place of worship. It was a picture of heaven itself and of God's throne.

As you entered the tabernacle, you'd first come to a section called the Holy Place. Beyond the Holy Place was one more area that could be entered: the Holy of Holies. Only the high priest could enter this innermost chamber, and he did so, typically, once a year.

When the high priest entered the Holy of Holies, he carried a golden censer filled with super-hot coals. He would place crushed incense on these burning coals, and the incense would immediately burn up, flooding the Holy of Holies with a sweet-smelling smoke.

There are symbolic attributes to this that everyone who studies the Bible needs to understand. In Old Testament times, when people needed to hear from God, they went through the prophets. When they needed to speak to God, they went through the priests.

The priest would enter the Holy of Holies with the censer, coals, and incense. The smoke, representing all the prayers of the saints, would fill the Holy of Holies, and God would hear the prayers of His people. They understood that when God's people cry out to Him in prayer, He receives them as a sweet-smelling fragrance.

A massive veil separated the Holy of Holies, where only the priests could enter, from the Holy Place. According to Jewish tradition, it was a "handbreadth," or about four inches thick, and so heavy that it would have taken several hundred priests to move it.

This is another powerful example of how the Old and New Testaments come to life together. Matthew 27:51 tells us that when Christ was crucified and gave up His last breath, the temple veil was torn from top to bottom. Because of this, everyone who puts their faith in Christ, our High Priest from the line of Judah, born after the order of Melchizedek, now has direct access to God! Every time you pray to the LORD, whether in your car, your kitchen, or anywhere else, it rises to Him as a sweet-smelling fragrance. We have an open door to Him!

We see this beautifully illustrated in Revelation 8:3, where the angel with a golden censer offers up the prayers of the saints, just as we saw earlier in Revelation 5:8. The saints who were not raptured, those who didn't believe in the LORD until after the rapture, are dying because of persecution from the Antichrist. They cry out, "LORD, when are You going to avenge this death?" And the LORD receives their prayers like a fragrance.

As a matter of fact, the next verse shows us exactly what happens with this burning incense, and it will literally shake the world.

God's Judgment Begins

"And the angel took the censer, and filled it with fire of the altar, and cast it into the earth: and there were voices, and thunderings, and lightnings, and an earthquake."

Revelation 8:5

After reading this verse , I feel compelled to direct your attention to Leviticus 16:12-13, which reads, "And he shall take a censer full of burning coals of fire from off the altar before the LORD, and his hands full of sweet incense beaten small, and bring it within the veil. And he shall put the incense upon the fire before the LORD, that the cloud of the incense may cover the mercy seat that is upon the testimony, that he die not." What you're reading is an act that took place on Yom Kippur, otherwise known as the Day of Atonement. On that day, the high priest would take his censer filled with coals from the altar to burn incense before the LORD.

In Revelation Chapter 8, I can't help but see this angel perform a similar act. He offers incense with the prayers of the saints, and I want you to remember the parallels I drew between the prayers of the saints and the sweet-smelling savor before the LORD. Those prayers are then taken and transformed into a mechanism of judgment, just as that same censer becomes an instrument of judgment.

This connection highlights a profound shift, and I need you to understand it. What was once a means of atonement and intercession has now, as a result of humanity's hardness of heart and rejection of God, become an instrument of wrath. The same fire that purifies and sanctifies the righteous will also destroy the rebellious.

> "And the seven angels which had the seven trumpets prepared themselves to sound."
>
> **Revelation 8:6**

When the last seal is opened, it introduces the next set of judgments. The seven angels with trumpets prepare to sound. And what happens when the first trumpet blows is astonishing.

> "The first angel sounded, and there followed hail and fire mingled with blood, and they were cast upon the earth: and the third part of trees was burnt up, and all green grass was burnt up."
>
> **Revelation 8:7**

The irony of today's massive climate change narrative isn't lost on me here. So-called experts, celebrities, and political leaders, like the governor of California, basically worship the earth. They'll shut down fishermen to save some obscure shark nobody's ever heard of. It's honestly dark and evil.

Look, I'm all for taking care of the world God has given us. Christians have a responsibility to be good stewards of the earth, but within reason. We shouldn't worship the world because God is its Creator, and we don't worship His creation, we worship Him.

We should also keep in mind that one day God will indeed burn a third of the world. That doesn't give us some twisted justification to be careless or poor stewards of what He's entrusted to us. But it does remind us to keep everything in proper perspective, understanding that all of it rests in God's hands and that only He is worthy of our worship.

When the first trumpet sounds and signals God's judgment, there will be fire like the world has never seen.

The Second and Third Trumpets

Pay attention to what takes place next:

"And the second angel sounded, and as it were a great mountain burning with fire was cast into the sea: and the third part of the sea became blood."

Revelation 8:8

Notice how many people worship the ocean today. It's crazy. But when we look back at biblical history, we see this isn't new. The Egyptians placed a premium on the Nile River. So when God judged them for holding His people in captivity, He turned the Nile's waters into blood. Another pattern: when God judges people for worshiping something other than Himself, He destroys what they worship, and often uses that very thing against them.

As I mentioned before, the ancient Egyptians worshiped a goddess called Heqet, who had the head of a frog. One of the plagues God delivered through Moses was frogs. And so many frogs emerged from the Nile that the Bible says they swarmed the land and filled every home and space, eventually becoming unbearable. Pharaoh finally begged, "Stop this. We can't take it. There are too many of them."

When God judges people who hate Him, He does it this exact way: "You want it? Okay, you can have it."

> "And the third part of the creatures which were in the sea, and had life, died; and the third part of the ships were destroyed."

Revelation 8:9

To those who want to worship the ocean because they think it will give them everything: God is going to wipe out a third of it and the creatures living in it. And because of the people's disobedience to God, the economy from the sea will be decimated.

> "And the third angel sounded, and there fell a great star from heaven, burning as it were a lamp, and it fell upon the third part of the rivers, and upon the fountains of waters; And the name of the star is called Wormwood: and the third part of the waters became wormwood; and many men died of the waters, because they were made bitter."

Revelation 8:10–11

I don't believe for one second that the name Wormwood assigned to the star that falls is a coincidence. This isn't just some random name chosen to illustrate bitterness in the fresh waters. It goes far deeper than that. I actually believe this is a powerful demonstration of a principle found in the Book of Jeremiah.

In Jeremiah Chapters 9 and 23, we read: "And the LORD saith, Because they have forsaken my law which I set before them, and have not obeyed my voice, neither walked therein;

But have walked after the imagination of their own heart, and after Baalim, which their fathers taught them: Therefore thus saith the LORD of hosts, the God of Israel; Behold, I will feed them, even this people, with wormwood, and give them water of gall to drink" (Jeremiah 9:13–15). And again: "Therefore thus saith the LORD of hosts concerning the prophets; Behold, I will feed them with wormwood, and make them drink the water of gall: for from the prophets of Jerusalem is profaneness gone forth into all the land" (Jeremiah 23:15).

As you can see, Jeremiah uses wormwood, a bitter plant that many readers may not recognize, as a powerful symbol of divine judgment. In Jeremiah's context, God confronts spiritual corruption and moral decay with this imagery. In that day, it led to deeply physical consequences.

Here in Revelation, the wormwood causes people to drink bitterness as a result of rejecting God's Word. John's vision builds directly on Jeremiah's ominous and prophetic imagery, expanding it to a global scale. What was once a national judgment on Israel now becomes a judgment upon the entire world that rejected Israel and Israel's God.

The Fourth Trumpet

> "And the fourth angel sounded, and the third part of the sun was smitten, and the third part of the moon, and the third part of the stars; so as the third part of them was darkened, and the day shone not for a third part of it, and the night likewise."

Revelation 8:12

Picture what it will be like: skies filled with thunder and

lightning, the earth rocked by a massive earthquake, followed by a third of the oceans dying and a third of the world's fresh water poisoned. Then the sun, the moon, and a third of the stars will go dark. It is beyond sad.

Much like many of today's disasters, caused by poor management and overregulation that end up destroying the natural conservation God designed, the world is going to suffer on a completely different scale. Once again, this is a picture that aptly demonstrates what happens when you worship creation and ignore the Creator: the consequence is devastating.

The very thing you worship reveals itself to be as fragile as it truly is, because as creation, it can never do what only the Creator can do. That's why this judgment is so meaningful and why it should speak so clearly to us.

It speaks directly to the pattern in God's judgment, where He simply says, "I will execute your punishment by giving you the very thing you demand. I will leave you to yourself to experience the consequence of the foolish decisions you have chosen to make."

> "And I beheld, and heard an angel flying through the midst of heaven, saying with a loud voice, Woe, woe, woe, to the inhabiters of the earth by reason of the other voices of the trumpet of the three angels, which are yet to sound!"
>
> **Revelation 8:13**

That's heavy. Imagine just having gone through all of that and then witnessing an angel flying overhead and hearing a voice that the entire world can hear: "Woe, woe, woe!" One woe for each of the remaining trumpets.

King Charles III has spoken about the earth numerous times. But his statement at COP28 in Dubai in December 2023 may have been one of his most alarming: "The Earth does not belong to us, we belong to the Earth." Sorry, King Charles! God's going to judge it, and the same earth you worship will be the very first thing destroyed. That's what happens when we place anything above God.

The Way Sin Works

It's the way sin works, folks. It's the way wickedness operates. I say this to pastors all the time: "Stand up and fight against the evils of the day, because if you don't, you'll be the first victim of those evils. They will come for you first." For those who embrace and peddle wokeness, I promise, the woke industrial complex will come for them before anyone else. Why? Because evil always ends up destroying itself. The enemy thought he killed Jesus on the cross. Instead, Christ sacrificed Himself and conquered death through His own resurrection, taking the keys of hell!

This is the message I want to get across. Please listen and hear my heart. What we're about to read next describes hell literally breaking loose on earth. If you think what we've just studied is bad, you haven't seen anything yet.

Hold fast to the LORD. Stay close to the Word of God. Make it part of you. Study it and let God's Word show you how to live daily. Let it guide everything you do, fundamentally and foundationally, in every area of your life. God's Word will inspire you. It will build you up and give you the direction you need.

Because without it, we have nothing.

Why God's Wrath Is Just

I often get asked: "How can God be just in pouring out such wrath?"

God's wrath is completely justified, and here's why: it's never arbitrary or impulsive. Everything we see in these trumpet judgments flows directly from mankind's deliberate rejection of God and their choice to worship creation instead of the Creator. God doesn't force anyone to rebel against Him. He doesn't make anyone choose evil over good. His judgment consistently involves giving people exactly what they think they want, and then letting them experience the full consequences of that choice.

What This Means for Us Today

So what does this mean for us as believers living in these last days? Several things:

First, we need to recognize that we're living in a time of God's patience, not His indifference. The fact that these judgments haven't come yet doesn't mean God doesn't see the wickedness around us. It means He's being patient, not willing that any should perish but that all should come to repentance (2 Peter 3:9). But that patience has limits.

Second, we need to actively engage in being the restraining force God has called us to be. Christians are the preserving influence in this world. In Matthew 5:13, Jesus calls His followers "the salt of the earth." We're meant to prevent moral and spiritual decay by upholding righteous, Christlike living and being a positive influence on society. When we refuse to stand against evil and choose silence in the face of wickedness, we abdicate our God-given responsibility and invite judgment.

Third, we need to understand that the current trajectory of our culture, the worship of environmentalism over the Creator, the elevation of human wisdom over divine revelation, and the celebration of sin as virtue) is setting the stage for exactly the kind of judgment we read about in Revelation Chapter 8.

Just look around you. We live in a society that worships everything except the true God. Just like the ancient Egyptians of Moses's time and every other society that has chosen this path, judgment is coming.

The Mercy in the Wrath

But even in these terrible judgments, we see God's mercy. Notice that it's only a third of the trees, a third of the sea, a third of the fresh water. God has always restrained His full wrath, and He will again. Even in judgment, He provides many opportunities for repentance.

The angel flying through heaven crying "Woe, woe, woe" isn't celebrating destruction. It's issuing a warning. God is saying, "There's still time to repent. Turn back to Me." That's the heart of a loving God, even amid righteous judgment. He doesn't delight in the death of the wicked. His desire is that they turn from their wickedness and live.

So how should we respond to this knowledge?

For the Non-believer: Understand that these judgments are coming, and the only way to escape them is through faith in Jesus Christ. The church will be raptured before these things happen, but if you reject Christ now, you'll face them head-on.

Don't wait. Don't think you can just decide later not to take the mark of the beast. If you won't stand for Christ now in the easy times, you certainly won't stand for Him when your life depends on it.

For the Believer: Understand that we have work to do. We can't just sit back and wait for the rapture while the world goes to hell around us. We are called to be salt and light, to be the restraining force, to stand against evil, and proclaim righteousness.

For Everyone: The silence in heaven that opens Revelation Chapter 8 should remind us that there are times when God's longsuffering gives way to righteous anger. We are living in the last moments of His patience with this world. The trumpet judgments show us what happens when His patience finally ends, what the world will look like when God removes His hand of protection and gives people what they've chosen.

The trumpet judgments also show us the incredible mercy we've already received. Though we deserve God's judgment, we can be saved by grace through faith in Jesus.

The Ultimate Hope

The silence in heaven is only temporary. The trumpet judgments, as terrible as they are, aren't the end of the story. They're birth pangs, preparing the world for the return of the righteous King. They're the darkness before the dawn of Christ's millennial reign, which will culminate in a new heaven and a new earth, void of all that is evil. God is both perfectly just and perfectly merciful. His wrath is righteous because sin deserves judgment. But His mercy is abundant because He provided a way of escape through His Son's death on the cross.

Let us be motivated not to fear, but to action. Let us embrace and proclaim the Gospel with urgency. Let us live holy lives that shine as lights in this dark world.

God's love for us stretches as far as the east is from the west. And His Word is true. That's the hope that sustains us as we watch these dark days unfold. That's the truth that gives us courage to stand firm until the end.

9
Trumpets of Terror

Before we dive into Revelation Chapter 9, let's start with Revelation 8:13. Chapter and verse designations sometimes require us to look backward to understand what's coming next.

One theme that keeps flowing through the Book of Revelation is this: Praise God that we won't be here. I mean it. When you look at what's happening now, what we're going to face, and the description of what lies ahead, it's not going to be pretty. It's comforting, almost cathartic, to recognize that we won't be on this earth when these things unfold, that this won't be an issue for us. I'm deeply grateful for that because the judgment described here is ugly. It's not pleasant.

King James language can throw us off because we sometimes miss words designed to be super emphatic, because we don't understand the world that language came from.

"And I beheld, and heard an angel flying through the midst of heaven, saying with a loud voice, Woe, woe, woe, to the inhabiters of the earth by reason of the other voices of the trumpet of the three angels, which are yet to sound!"

Revelation 8:13

When we see this emphatic triple woe, it signals something beyond disaster. It speaks of divinely inspired calamity, designed to create a sobering awareness of the chain of events that led to it. This is no casual warning. The angels' lament on behalf of God declares what's about to unfold in the most catastrophic way imaginable, and then some.

We see a striking parallel to this in the Old Testament when we read Isaiah Chapter 5. God, through His prophet Isaiah, pronounced a series of woes upon His people because they had rebelled against Him. "Woe unto them that join house to house, that lay field to field, till there be no place, that they may be placed alone in the midst of the earth... Woe unto them that rise up early in the morning, that they may follow strong drink... Woe unto them that call evil good, and good evil; that put darkness for light, and light for darkness; that put bitter for sweet, and sweet for bitter." (Isaiah 5:8, 11, 20)

Pay attention to the woes expressed in Isaiah because they speak to the very same issues summoning God's judgment here in the Book of Revelation. We're seeing corruption, moral decay, and spiritual blindness, all of which called for God's judgment then and are calling for it now. The earth trembles because this judgment surpasses anything witnessed in human history.

Make no mistake: this is a globalized, far more catastrophic version of judgment than anything we saw in the Book of Isaiah. It expresses finality and demands that we pause once again to praise God that we will not be here during this time.

The Bottomless Pit Opens

"And the fifth angel sounded, and I saw a star fall from heaven unto the earth: and to him was given the key of the bottomless pit. And he opened the bottomless pit; and there arose a smoke out of the pit, as the smoke of a great furnace; and the sun and the air were darkened by reason of the smoke of the pit."

Revelation 9:1–2

Picture this like a massive volcanic eruption in terms of the smoke billowing out. But let me be clear: this pit isn't a volcano. It's actually a holding tank for deeply evil, wicked, demonic creatures. What we're reading here is neither pleasant nor metaphorical.

We're talking about a very literal set of circumstances. These descriptions are real. They speak to something tangible and actual. I want everyone to understand that what we're seeing here is meant to be taken literally.

Now, let me pause for a moment to reflect on something important. In the United States especially, we struggle to discern spiritual things. Why? Because we've chosen to ignore them. We've allowed ourselves to become so absorbed in our own desires and indulgences that we sacrifice our salvation, our minds, our hearts, our sanity. We're willing to deny the truth just so we can keep feeding our appetites.

When someone tells me they're an atheist, I don't think they're truly atheist. A real atheist wouldn't spend so much energy being angry at a god they claim doesn't exist. What they're actually revealing is that they worship their own intellect or something other than the true and living God. Something in their life has taken God's position.

In America, this takes many forms. For some, it's physical gratification in the form of sex, drugs, alcohol, or other addictions. Others worship material gain and the pursuit of money. The specific idol doesn't matter. Every human being that has ever existed, and everyone who will exist, defaults to worshiping something. I can say this definitively because God created mankind with a purpose, and that purpose is clearly tied to worship. When we redirect that purpose toward anything outside God's design, we're worshiping something other than what He intended. The consequences of that choice are disastrous.

Our default position is to be devoted to something, and whatever captures our greatest attention becomes, in essence, what we worship. The question that carries profound consequence is this: what are you worshiping? Understanding the answer is critical because your standing in eternity depends on it.

We spend so much time numbing our minds and hearts to what God wants, pursuing other things we've elevated to objects of worship, especially in Western civilization. Many have lost touch with the things of God and no longer discern what carries true spiritual meaning. So when we read the Book of Revelation, we often dismiss books like this as simply metaphorical.

The Great Misinterpretation

As I've mentioned before, one of the grave errors in reading the Book of Revelation is assuming that virtually everything has some metaphorical meaning, that the terminology sounds antiquated and must be symbolic. Nothing could be further from the truth. This chapter is particularly subject to this misreading, which leads to interpretations that completely miss what's critical.

Here's a prime example: many pastors in recent years have conflated this chapter with Revelation 16, and as a result, they believe we're talking about a human army, specifically China. Some of the most respected Bible prophecy teachers have popularized this idea, but again, nothing could be further from the truth. I should probably give you a spoiler alert: the army we're about to read about is actually a horde of demons, not a human army. That fact bears significant consequence, because it speaks to a much deeper issue we're about to discuss.

Another reason people interpret these passages this way is that they've become callused to understanding the spiritual. When John described what he was seeing, he was simply limited by the terminology of his time. He was witnessing things no one in his time had ever seen before. But understand this: he's not talking about technology or military equipment like airplanes or helicopters. He's describing something he'd never encountered before, something with a spiritual character, a spiritual being.

So when you read about this bottomless pit with smoke pouring out so thick it darkens the sky, we're not reading about a volcano, although a volcano can do that. John is describing an actual holding place for some very evil, wicked, demonic creatures.

Demonic Locusts Unleashed

> "And there came out of the smoke locusts upon the earth: and unto them was given power, as the scorpions of the earth have power."

Revelation 9:3

Now, this is interesting. Several kinds of scorpions are indigenous to different parts of the United States. In Arizona alone, there are 56 species of scorpions. And while less than 1% of scorpions worldwide have venom capable of killing a human, they can cause tremendous pain. If you've ever been stung by a scorpion, you know exactly how painful it is. The point here is that this locust creature has the power to inflict pain; "as the scorpion has power."

And it gets way worse:

> "And it was commanded them that they should not hurt the grass of the earth, neither any green thing, neither any tree; but only those men which have not the seal of God in their foreheads."

Revelation 9:4

So if you're not marked by God, these locust creatures, possessing the power to sting like scorpions, are instructed to attack you. What's also interesting is they won't eat grass or any green thing. Normally, swarms of locusts consume vegetation, wiping out everything in their path. But these creatures will do only one thing: attack people who don't have God's seal protecting them. Anyone who isn't part of the 144,000 is in big trouble.

The Torment That Makes Men Seek Death

"And to them it was given that they should not kill them, but that they should be tormented five months: and their torment was as the torment of a scorpion, when he striketh a man."

Revelation 9:5

Think about that for a second. People will get hit with pain so severe, they'll actually want to die.

"And in those days shall men seek death, and shall not find it; and shall desire to die, and death shall flee from them."

Revelation 9:6

In a time when we spend unfathomable resources searching for ways to cheat death, the thought that mankind will one day seek death seems strange. I have a good friend whose father was the oldest man in the United States when he died at 113 years old. Many people would trade their fortunes to live that long or go back and add 20 years to their lives.

Yet during the season described in verse six, many will wish for their lives to end with the same desperation people today show when trying to extend them. They'll want to die and won't be able to.

The Description of Demonic Creatures

"And the shapes of the locusts were like unto horses prepared unto battle; and on their heads were as it were crowns like gold, and their faces were as the faces of men. And they had hair as the hair of women, and their teeth were as the teeth of lions. And they had breastplates, as it were breastplates of iron: and the sound of their wings was as the sound of chariots of many horses running to battle. And they had tails like unto scorpions, and there were stings in their tails: and their power was to hurt men five months."

Revelation 9:7–10

Many Bible teachers claim this passage describes some type of modern aircraft. In fact, I recently heard someone insist it was the perfect description of a Sikorsky helicopter. Someone else told me, "No, no, this verse describes an Apache helicopter." I heard another pastor talk about an old commentator who claimed this passage perfectly describes a bomber airplane because the gun placement on those aircraft resembled a "tail that stings." While some make a somewhat convincing argument that this could be military hardware, the reality is there's no way it's a man-made item. This is a demonic creature. And I can prove it.

Consider this: even with the massive effort to build planes during World War II, the US only produced about 300,000 aircraft. If we ordered a million planes, jets, or helicopters from the largest manufacturers today, it would take several decades to deliver that quantity.

To add perspective, the history of aviation spans over 120 years, with production spikes during world wars and the Cold War. Based on data from production lists, aviation databases (e.g., Military Factory, Statista), and industry reports, the estimate for the total number of aircraft ever produced is between 600,000 to 700,000 worldwide. And this figure includes commercial, military, and general aviation. The idea of organizing two hundred million vehicles for a coordinated military effort, and then supplying the fuel, infrastructure, and logistical support required to operate them, is physically and practically impossible.

I believe without question that God can speak an army of any size into existence at any time. There's no limit to His power, but we must understand the language in this chapter isn't describing a human army composed of machines, but a supernatural horde beyond human ability or comprehension. The Bible describes actual demons. That fact bears significant consequence for how we understand what is coming.

With all that said, let's return to the Book of Revelation. We're not talking about one million. We're talking about 200 times that, a staggering number. It's logistically and physically impossible to coordinate 200 million people in a military effort of this scale.

The King of Destruction

> "And they had a king over them, which is the angel of the bottomless pit, whose name in the Hebrew tongue is Abaddon, but in the Greek tongue hath his name Apollyon."
>
> **Revelation 9:11**

Both Abaddon and Apollyon translate to "destruction." If verse 11 is talking about the devil, and it is, then the devil is aptly named. In other words, the only purpose of this king is to destroy.

"One woe is past; and, behold, there come two woes more hereafter."

Revelation 9:12

Can you imagine how ugly these creatures working alongside the devil are? They're not like some common everyday locust you take out with a fly swatter and say, "Bye-bye." They are not little pests. They are not military machines. They are demonic.

The Army of 200 Million

"And the sixth angel sounded, and I heard a voice from the four horns of the golden altar which is before God, saying to the sixth angel which had the trumpet, Loose the four angels which are bound in the great river Euphrates. And the four angels were loosed, which were prepared for an hour, and a day, and a month, and a year, for to slay the third part of men."

Revelation 9:13–15

Consider these numbers for a moment as we look at the massive loss of life described here. For this demonstration, let's assume that after the rapture takes place, when all believers are taken up with Christ, four billion people remain on earth.

In Revelation Chapter 6, when the fourth seal breaks, a quarter of the world's population dies. That's one billion people gone, leaving three billion. Then, when the judgment in Revelation Chapter 9 occurs, a third of the remaining population is destroyed, another billion people, leaving just two billion people on Earth.

Let's start with six billion people instead. Twenty-five percent die, that's one and a half billion, leaving four and a half billion. Then one third of those die, another one and a half billion, leaving three billion.

If we begin with eight billion, two billion would die first, leaving six billion. Then another two billion would die, leaving four billion. Starting with twelve billion? Three billion would die first, leaving nine billion, and then another three billion would die, leaving six billion.

No matter which scenario we consider, the loss of life is staggering. But for our discussion, let's return to the original case: we start with four billion and end with only two billion people left on Earth.

That means with just two billion people remaining and 200 million of these creatures on the loose, there's one of them for every ten human beings. It's mind-boggling to think about the devastation.

> "And the number of the army of the horsemen were two hundred thousand thousand: and I heard the number of them."
>
> **Revelation 9:16**

That's the number: "Two hundred thousand thousand" or 200 million. And even if you assumed these were 200 million human soldiers, the logistics alone make it impossible. Anyone with a military or logistics background knows it's absurd to think you could move and sustain a force that massive.

China may claim to have an army of 100 million men, which is where some people get their mistaken idea that the Bible describes human soldiers, but it simply doesn't work. And God Himself makes it clear that's not what we're dealing with.

Fire, Smoke, and Brimstone

"And thus I saw the horses in the vision, and them that sat on them, having breastplates of fire, and of jacinth, and brimstone: and the heads of the horses were as the heads of lions; and out of their mouths issued fire and smoke and brimstone. By these three was the third part of men killed, by the fire, and by the smoke, and by the brimstone, which issued out of their mouths. For their power is in their mouth, and in their tails: for their tails were like unto serpents, and had heads, and with them they do hurt."

Revelation 9:17–19

Now, pay close attention to what came out of their mouths. The text says it was "by the fire, by the smoke, and by the brimstone." Some people might say, "These sound like missiles coming out of a helicopter." But John didn't say it was like fire and like smoke and like brimstone. He says it was fire, smoke, and brimstone. He's describing something he knew and understood.

People will be killed by the fire, smoke, and brimstone. And it will be absolutely terrible.

The Heart That Will Not Repent

"And the rest of the men which were not killed by these

plagues yet repented not of the works of their hands, that they should not worship devils, and idols of gold, and silver, and brass, and stone, and of wood: which neither can see, nor hear, nor walk: Neither repented they of their murders, nor of their sorceries, nor of their fornication, nor of their thefts."

Revelation 9:20–21

What a terrible picture. Think about this: the whole world is being destroyed by the hand of God. The people in the midst of it, watching it unfold, will know it's coming from God. Yet they refuse to repent. Their willful desire to live according to the lust of their flesh and continue in sin causes them to wave their fists in rebellion toward God.

What troubles me most as I read about ancient biblical times is how people who worshiped false gods made statues commemorating it. They knew full well what they were doing and were openly brazen about it. In a way, that may have worked to their advantage. The propensity to repent was perhaps a little higher because they knew exactly what they were doing. But today, an overwhelming majority of people don't even realize they're engaging in spiritual activity. Many continue rejecting God and worshiping the idols in their lives without fully recognizing what they're actually doing.

Have you ever met somebody addicted to drugs? It's incredibly sad and frustrating. They know they're destroying themselves, yet they keep doing it. I've never met someone hooked on drugs who didn't know what they were doing was harming them. And most of them don't understand the spiritual significance of it. I've told people, "You know you need to stop using drugs." They'll say, "I know, man, I want to stop."

Even when I tell them, "But you understand you're participating in witchcraft," I almost always get the response: "No, I'm not. I'm not into any of that stuff. Oh, you're crazy." They are, but they don't recognize the spiritual element of what they're actually doing. Here in the United States and in many other parts of the world, people continue participating in evil, demonic things without seeing that they're engaging in spiritual activity. They don't see it as sin. That's scary, and it's terribly sad.

A Final Warning

I was talking to someone I love and admire, but he doesn't know the LORD. He pulled me aside and said, "You know, James, you spend a lot of time talking about negative things, all the bad stuff happening in the world." Then he added, "I read a great book I want to recommend to you." I said, "Okay." He continued, "The premise is that if you look at what's going on today, literally the moments we're in, including everything that happened with COVID, we're living a much better and more positive life than we ever have before in human history." I stood there thinking, what color is the sky right now in your world? What? There's no way anyone with reasonable observational skills could look at the world we're living in today and say it's a better day. It's not, it's a much worse day. We're warned in 2 Corinthians that the god of this world has blinded so many who don't know the LORD.

Folks, we cannot forget this. We cannot lose our understanding of this truth. There will come a point where people will continue to curse God, even when they know He's judging them. That's why it breaks my heart when someone says,

"James, I'm just going to wait until after the rapture. I'll be alright, I'm not going to take the mark." It doesn't work that way, my friends. If you won't stand against evil now, what makes you think you'll stand against it when there's a gun to your head? It's not going to happen.

I am earnestly pleading with you. If you've watched me online or listened to me on the radio, and you don't know the LORD, don't wait until the rapture takes place. When we walk in obedience to God, there's a great reward for it. God honors our obedience and He's glorified by it. There's too much at stake. Don't wait. Seek the LORD now. Walk with Him today.

10
A Bitter-Sweet Scroll

As we continue our journey through the Book of Revelation, we encounter one of the most fascinating interludes in this prophetic masterpiece. Before we dive into the specifics of Chapter 10, it's important to understand the pattern that has emerged throughout our study. We've seen this rhythm before: seals followed by an interlude, trumpets followed by another pause. This isn't random, it's the deliberate design of how God executes His judgment, with an ebb and flow that reveals both His justice and His mercy.

Think of it like waves on the ocean. There's a natural rhythm, a measurable delta between the peaks and valleys. When I use the term "delta," I'm referring to that measurable distance from the top of the wave to the bottom, how extreme the movements are in God's unfolding plan.

This mathematical precision isn't coincidental. Mathematics is a creation of God, built into our very DNA, woven into the fabric of language itself, and embedded in the prophetic structure of Scripture.

We've witnessed the opening of all seven seals, each

revealing another aspect of God's righteous judgment upon the earth. We've heard six of the seven trumpets blow, each bringing increasingly severe consequences for a rebellious world. Now, as we stand on the precipice of the seventh and final trumpet, God provides another interlude, another moment to catch our breath and understand what's unfolding.

This pattern reflects something deeply theological: God's judgments never come without warning, and they never come without pause for reflection. Even in His wrath, He remembers mercy. Even as He executes justice, He provides moments of clarity for those who have eyes to see and ears to hear.

With that said, I think it's really important to pause and take in the interlude we're about to enter as we go through this chapter. As the Book of Revelation has consistently demonstrated, there are striking parallels to the Old Testament. When it comes to these pauses that happen before God executes judgment, we see powerful examples throughout the Old Testament that confirm His character is consistent and His ways of judgment are always the same.

Even the pauses reveal God's heart. They show that He longs to extend mercy to people who desperately need it, even though they continue to raise their fists in open rebellion against Him. One such pause, coming both after judgment and before the execution of more judgment, can be found in Exodus 34:5. The Bible says, "And the LORD descended in the cloud, and stood with him there, and proclaimed the name of the LORD." This happened right after Israel had sinned by creating the golden calf. God stopped the forward movement of judgment and called Moses into His presence.

There's a reason for that pause. It allowed God to deal with sin thoroughly, preventing its destructive influence from spreading further. Between God's wrath and the opportunity He gives Israel for restoration, there's a divine interlude we cannot afford to miss. In that moment, Moses intercedes for the people, God reaffirms His covenant, and then, in an act of grace and mercy, He reveals His glory. The pause becomes a moment of revelation rather than the aftermath of destruction. This is exactly what we're seeing in Revelation Chapter 10. The pause between the sixth and seventh trumpet is a moment of glory, a recommissioning, and a reaffirmation of God's authority before He executes the next wave of judgment.

In the way, this same pattern appears in several other places throughout the Old Testament. In Habakkuk Chapter 3, we see a vision that bridges judgment and mercy. The prophet writes, "O LORD, I have heard thy speech, and was afraid: O LORD, revive thy work in the midst of the years, in the midst of the years make known; in wrath remember mercy" (Habakkuk 3:2). In Joshua Chapter 5, just before the battle of Jericho, the Commander of the LORD's army appears to Joshua. "And he said, Nay; but as captain of the host of the LORD am I now come. And Joshua fell on his face to the earth, and did worship" (Joshua 5:14). Then in 1 Kings Chapter 19, Elijah stands on Mount Horeb after the judgment that fell upon the prophets of Baal. The Bible says, "And after the fire a still small voice. And it was so, when Elijah heard it, that he wrapped his face in his mantle" (1 Kings 19:12–13).

Each of these moments reveals the same divine pattern we see in Revelation Chapter 10. God pauses between acts of judgment to reveal His glory, reaffirm His authority, and extend His mercy once again. Understanding this pattern adds tremendous value, and it shows that God's desire has always been to intervene with mercy, love, grace, and another opportunity for redemption.

The Mighty Angel Appears

With that foundation established, let's turn our attention to the first verse:

> "And I saw another mighty angel come down from heaven, clothed with a cloud, and a rainbow was upon his head, and his face was as it were the sun, and his feet as pillars of fire."

Revelation 10:1

I know many excellent Bible teachers, men with far more experience than I have, who look at this description and immediately conclude we're talking about Christ Himself. I understand their reasoning, and I'm not dismissing the possibility outright, but I'm not ready to make that assumption for several important reasons.

If this were Christ, I believe John would have immediately identified Him as such, just as he did in Revelation Chapter 1 when he described his vision of the glorified Jesus. John was the disciple closest to Jesus during His earthly ministry. He would have recognized his LORD immediately and said so explicitly. The fact that John calls this figure "another mighty angel" suggests we're dealing with a high-ranking angelic being with tremendous authority, but not Christ Himself.

With that said, the description is remarkable. This angel

comes clothed with a cloud, and we find a powerful Old Testament parallel from Israel's early history when a cloud was associated with God's presence and glory. During the day, the LORD appeared as a pillar of cloud to lead His people, guiding them step by step through the wilderness (Exodus 13:21–22). Similarly, the cloud that rested over the tabernacle represented His continual presence and direction (Exodus 40:34–38).

Even in the New Testament, clouds remain connected to Christ's presence, at His ascension and in His promised return. The angel clothed with a cloud in Revelation signals divine guidance and authority, revealing that the message comes directly from the LORD.

The rainbow on his head recalls the covenant promise God first made after the flood in Noah's day (Genesis 9:12–17). It represents God's faithfulness, assuring us that even as He brings judgment upon a rebellious world, that judgment won't fall on those who turn to Him in repentance, even during this time of great tribulation.

His face shining like the sun and his feet like pillars of fire echo the radiance of divine glory, the same glory we see at Mount Sinai, where God's presence descended in fire and smoke (Exodus 19:18), at the Mount of Transfiguration, and at the very throne of God. Whether this being is Christ Himself or a mighty angel sent with His full authority, one thing is certain: he carries the presence, power, and message of Almighty God.

A Declaration of Dominion

"And he had in his hand a little open book, and he set

his right foot upon the sea, and his left foot upon the earth, and he cried with a loud voice, as when a lion roaring."

Revelation 10:2

The symbolism here is unmistakable. This being places one foot on the sea and one foot on the land, claiming dominion over everything that has ever caused mankind fear or anxiety. In John's day, the sea represented the great unknown, the final frontier that terrified sailors and travelers. By placing his feet on both sea and earth, this mighty angel (or Christ Himself) declares: "I have authority over everything that causes you fear. I am speaking to you with the full authority of God Almighty."

The little book in his hand is open, not sealed like the scroll we saw earlier. This suggests that what's about to be revealed is meant to be understood, at least in part. The timing is significant. We're standing at the threshold of the final trumpet, the culmination of God's judgment, and new revelation is being given.

Yet what we're seeing here isn't something new in the sense of being newly conceived. God is once again revealing through John something that has been divinely hardwired into the very construct of the Old Testament. The realization that follows is remarkable: this isn't a message made up on the fly. Rather, it's something woven into the fabric of God's plan from the very beginning.

It reflects a calculated and intricate design that has always demonstrated His consistency, His sovereignty, and His desire to extend love and grace to His people. When this mighty being cries out with a loud voice, as when a lion roars, the very heavens respond, marking one of the most intriguing and awe-inspiring moments in all of God's revelation.

The Seven Thunders

"And when he had cried, seven thunders uttered their voices. And when the seven thunders had uttered their voices, I was about to write, and I heard a voice from heaven saying unto me, Seal up those things which the seven thunders uttered, and write them not."

Revelation 10:3–4

Here we encounter something unprecedented in John's prophetic experience. Throughout Revelation, John has faithfully recorded everything he sees and hears. It's become his pattern, his spiritual discipline. When God speaks, John writes it down. But here, for the first time, he's commanded to do the opposite.

People often ask me, "What did the seven thunders say? What was this mysterious message?" The answer is beautifully simple: I don't know. Neither do you. And neither does anyone else, despite what various teachers might claim.

This isn't a failure of biblical scholarship or a gap in our understanding that we need to fill with speculation. It's intentional. God commanded John not to record these words, which means He doesn't want us to know what they were, at least not yet.

Some teachers tie these seven thunders to the seven spirits of God or other biblical numerological systems, but such attempts are misguided and potentially misleading.

If God wanted us to know what the thunders proclaimed, He would have told John to write it down. Since He explicitly forbade it, we must resist the temptation to speculate. Rather than seeing this as frustrating, we should see it as exciting. This sealed message reminds us of several profound truths:

First, it emphasizes the importance of recording God's voice when He speaks to us. John's immediate impulse was to write down what he heard. He understood the value of documenting divine revelation. As believers, we should cultivate this same habit. When God speaks to our hearts, when He gives us insight or direction, we need to write it down. Too many of us assume we'll remember these precious moments, but memory fails and circumstances change.

Second, the sealed nature of this message reminds us that God has far more in store for us than we can currently comprehend. We have so much to look forward to! The same God who told Daniel to seal up certain prophecies until the time of understanding has given us glimpses of coming glory that we can't yet fully comprehend.

Consider this: virtually none of the Old Testament prophets fully understood what they were writing. When Isaiah penned his detailed description of Christ's crucifixion in Isaiah Chapter 53, he wrote with such precision you'd think he witnessed the event firsthand. Yet he was describing something that wouldn't happen for another seven centuries. When Daniel recorded his visions of future kingdoms and end-times events, he was writing about things completely beyond his experience or understanding.

These men were told to write down things they couldn't

comprehend, knowing future generations would have the knowledge and context to make sense of their words. How exciting is that? We serve a God who reveals His mysteries progressively, giving us just enough light for the next step while promising greater understanding is still to come.

This is the wonder of walking with an infinite God. We'll never arrive at complete knowledge this side of eternity. We'll always be learning, always growing, always discovering new depths of His character and His ways. That's not a limitation, it's a promise of eternal adventure with our Creator.

I want to go back to something I mentioned earlier in this book. Remember when I said you'll become what you worship because that's how God designed us? Who we are always determines what we do, not the other way around. This truth connects directly to the truth that our identity in Christ shapes everything we encounter in life.

But there's a deeper issue at play here. There are times when God intentionally withholds information from us because He's developing within us the spiritual discipline of trusting Him when we don't understand all the variables involved in our decisions. I cannot emphasize enough how important it is to recognize that God requires us to put our full faith and trust in Him, even when we cannot see the whole picture.

One of the most dangerous things we can do as believers is to build a list of pros and cons as the basis for our obedience. The lesson we learn from the mystery of the seven thunders is that the only thing that matters is what God has told us to do. We don't need to understand everything He reveals, nor do we need to make sense of it in our limited reasoning, because we know He is infinitely wiser than we could ever be.

We must rest in the truth that He knows more than we do, which is why seeking to understand His will in the moment is far more important than trying to fill in the gaps of knowledge we were never meant to possess. Remember: there is only one true and living God, and we are not Him!

Time's Up

The mighty angel then makes a solemn declaration:

> "And [he] lifted up his hand to heaven, and sware by him that liveth for ever and ever, who created heaven, and the things that therein are, and the earth, and the things that therein are, and the sea, and the things which are therein, that there should be time no longer."

Revelation 10:5–6

This is a profound moment. The being swears by the eternal God, the Creator of all things, giving his oath the highest possible authority. Some argue this supports the idea that this is Christ Himself, since Hebrews tells us that God swears by His own name because there is nothing greater to swear by. Whether it's Christ or a mighty angel speaking with His full authority, the message carries the same weight.

But what does "time no longer" mean? I believe this is a poor translation that has caused unnecessary confusion. This doesn't mean God is about to destroy the dimension of time itself. Rather, it's a declaration that time is running out, that events are about to unfold rapidly and decisively. A better translation might be "time's up" or "no more delay."

This makes perfect sense in context. We're on the verge of the seventh trumpet, the culmination of God's judgment program. The angel is declaring that the period of delay, the season of God's patience, is coming to an end. What has been prophesied for millennia is about to happen, and it's going to happen quickly.

We've seen how rapidly things can change in recent years. Within weeks, the entire world shut down. Cities burned while authorities stood by. Freedoms we took for granted vanished overnight. If someone had told you three years ago that such dramatic changes could happen so quickly, you would have thought they were crazy. But we saw it with our own eyes.

This preview shows how quickly prophetic events can unfold. When God says "time's up," things happen fast. The angel's declaration serves as both warning and promise: a warning to those who continue in rebellion and a promise to those waiting for their redemption.

Mysteries Revealed

"But in the days of the voice of the seventh angel, when he shall begin to sound, the mystery of God should be finished, as he hath declared to his servants the prophets."

Revelation 10:7

This verse takes us back to something I mentioned earlier about the progressive nature of prophetic revelation. The word "mystery" here doesn't mean a puzzle to be solved through clever detective work. In biblical terms, a mystery is information you could never obtain through investigation or human reasoning, it can only be known through divine revelation.

Think about all those Old Testament prophets who wrote about events they couldn't possibly understand. They were recording mysteries, divine secrets that would only make sense when God chose to reveal their meaning. These men wrote down words they didn't fully grasp, described events beyond their comprehension, and recorded prophecies that wouldn't make sense for centuries or even millennia. But they remained faithful to write what God told them, trusting that He would reveal the meaning in His perfect timing.

Now, as we approach the sounding of the seventh trumpet, the angel declares that these mysteries, these long-sealed prophetic secrets, are about to be completed. The threads woven throughout Scripture are about to come together in a tapestry that will finally make complete sense.

The Bitter-Sweet Commission

Revelation Chapter 10 takes a personal turn as John receives a direct command:

> "And the voice which I heard from heaven spake unto me again, and said, Go and take the little book which is open in the hand of the angel which standeth upon the sea and upon the earth. And I went unto the angel, and said unto him, Give me the little book. And he said unto me, Take it, and eat it up; and it shall make thy belly bitter, but it shall be in thy mouth sweet as honey."

Revelation 10:8–9

Some teachers interpret this "eating" figuratively, suggesting it's like when we say we "devoured" a good book. But this misses the cultural context entirely. Figurative language like that wasn't part of the Greek or Aramaic mindset of that era. John literally ate this scroll, just as he describes. This might seem strange to us, but the symbolism runs deep.

It's important to take a closer look at what John is doing here, because the act of eating the little book is not without precedent. We see the same thing happen in the ministries of both Ezekiel and Jeremiah. In Ezekiel Chapter 3 we read, "Moreover he said unto me, Son of man, eat that thou findest; eat this roll, and go speak unto the house of Israel. So I opened my mouth, and he caused me to eat that roll. And he said unto me, Son of man, cause thy belly to eat, and fill thy bowels with this roll that I give thee. Then did I eat it; and it was in my mouth as honey for sweetness" (Ezekiel 3:1–3). In Jeremiah 15, the prophet writes, "Thy words were found, and I did eat them; and thy word was unto me the joy and rejoicing of mine heart: for I am called by thy name, O LORD God of hosts" (Jeremiah 15:16). I believe both Ezekiel and Jeremiah literally ate what they were told to eat, and that John did the same here. These were not symbolic gestures but literal acts designed to produce a profound spiritual effect, both in the prophets themselves and in those who would later study their obedience.

This act shows how God's Word should work in every believer's life. Two crucial lessons emerge from this. First, we must internalize God's Word before we can share it with others. We can't proclaim truth we haven't first absorbed and allowed to transform our own hearts. Second, as sweet as that internalization may be, it often turns bitter when we deliver it to others. The bitterness comes from people's rejection of God's Word, which stems from their unwillingness to abandon sin, a rebellion that always brings sorrow and ultimately destruction.

This is exactly why I believe John literally ate the little book. It drives home the same principle we see with Ezekiel and Jeremiah: God's Word is sweet to those who receive it but bitter to those who reject it. It reminds us that truth must first be absorbed before it can be proclaimed.

John continues:

"And I took the little book out of the angel's hand and ate it up; and it was in my mouth sweet as honey: and as soon as I had eaten it, my belly was bitter."

Revelation 10:10

Here we see the dual nature of prophetic truth: it's simultaneously sweet and bitter, comforting and convicting, encouraging and challenging. This perfectly captures every believer's experience with God's Word.

When we first encounter Scripture, it often tastes sweet to our spiritual palate. God's promises comfort us. His love encourages us. His plans for our future give us hope. The Word of God can be incredibly soothing, especially for those of us raised in it who find comfort in its familiar phrases and eternal truths.

But when we truly internalize God's Word, when it moves past the superficial level of hearing into the deep places of our innermost being, it often becomes bitter in our spiritual stomachs. Why? Because it convicts us. It confronts us and forces us to face truths about ourselves and our world that we'd rather avoid.

This is why I wrote earlier about internalizing God's Word and how it affects others when we proclaim it. The bitterness these prophets describe beautifully shows how God's Word works within us before it ever works through us. It must first be taken in, digested, and allowed to do its purifying work in the deepest parts of our hearts before God can use it to bring that same truth to others.

When we're born again, we first receive God's Word with sweetness, it fills us with hope, joy, and assurance. But as it begins to do its work in us, it often takes on a bitter quality because it exposes what's destructive, cleansing our hearts from the sin that corrupts. Yet for those who don't know the LORD at all, that same Word, once proclaimed by the one who has internalized it, been changed by it, and now speaks it, will be received as bitter from the start. To them, it becomes a message of judgment rather than life, because it confronts their rebellion and reveals their desperate need for repentance.

As a pastor, I can tell you there are passages of Scripture I simply don't enjoy teaching. Not because they're untrue or unimportant, but because God makes me internalize them as I prepare to share them. And when I internalize them, they stir me up, they convict me, challenge me, and force me to examine areas of my life I'd rather leave alone.

This is exactly what John experienced, and it's what every serious student of Bible prophecy experiences. The Word of God about future events is sweet when we first taste it.

We're excited about Christ's return, thrilled about our ultimate vindication, encouraged by the promise of justice and righteousness. But when we really digest it, when we think about what it means for our lost friends and family members, when we consider the judgment coming upon the earth, it becomes bitter in our stomachs.

John's experience with the scroll captures this dual reality. The prophecies he's about to proclaim will be sweet to those who love God's truth, but bitter as he contemplates the judgment coming upon rebellious humanity.

A Renewed Commission

Revelation Chapter 10 concludes with a renewed commission:

> "And he said unto me, Thou must prophesy again before many peoples, and nations, and tongues, and kings."

Revelation 10:11

This is significant. John has been prophesying throughout his vision, but now he receives a fresh mandate and a renewed commissioning for the work ahead. After internalizing this bitter-sweet revelation, after tasting both the sweetness of God's truth and the bitterness of coming judgment, John returns to his prophetic task with expanded scope and authority.

The phrase "prophesy again" carries a dual meaning here: continuation and renewal. John will continue his prophetic ministry, but with fresh understanding, deeper conviction, and broader reach. His message will extend to "many peoples, and nations, and tongues, and kings," The scope is global and the audience is universal.

This pattern holds true for every believer who seriously engages with God's Word. When we truly internalize Scripture, when we move past the sweetness of initial hearing into the deeper work of genuine transformation, we emerge changed, convicted, and recommissioned for service. We can't encounter the living Word of God and remain unchanged.

Lessons for Today

What can we learn from this remarkable chapter? Several crucial truths emerge:

First, we serve a God of patterns and precision. The mathematical precision we see in Revelation's structure reflects the character of our Creator, who has built order and beauty into every aspect of His creation. This should give us confidence in His prophetic Word. What God has promised, He will perform.

Second, God's timing is perfect. The interludes between judgments aren't delays or hesitations; they're deliberate pauses that serve divine purposes. Even in judgment, God shows mercy. Even in wrath, He provides opportunities for reflection and response.

Third, there's always more to learn about God. The sealed message of the seven thunders reminds us that our knowledge of God will continue expanding throughout eternity. We serve an infinite God, which means our relationship with Him will involve eternal growth, eternal discovery, eternal adventure.

Fourth, the Word of God should be both sweet and bitter

to us. If we're only experiencing the sweetness, we're probably not internalizing it deeply enough. If we're only experiencing the bitterness, we're missing the comfort and hope it provides. Healthy engagement with Scripture involves both dimensions.

Finally, serious and intentional engagement with God's Word leads to renewed commission. When we truly encounter divine truth, when we allow it to do its bitter-sweet work in our hearts, we emerge with a fresh mandate for service. The Word of God doesn't just inform us; it transforms us and recommissions us for kingdom work.

As we stand on the threshold of the seventh trumpet, we're reminded that time is short and the hour is late. The mysteries of God that have been hidden for ages are about to be revealed. The patience of God that has restrained judgment is about to give way to the final outpouring of His wrath.

But for those of us who belong to Christ, this isn't a cause for fear; it's a reason for excitement. We won't be here when the judgments come. We'll be safe in the presence of our LORD, watching as He completes His plan for the ages and establishes His kingdom on earth.

Time is running out, but for those who know Christ as Savior and LORD, the best is yet to come.

Conclusion

As we close this first book in my guide to Revelation series, my prayer is that the truths we've uncovered have drawn you nearer to the heart of Jesus Christ and stirred your spirit to live boldly in these last days. The LORD didn't give us the Book of Revelation to confuse or frighten us. He gave it to prepare us, to remind us who He is, what He's doing, and where all of this is headed. Every vision John saw was meant to pull back the veil and show us that heaven is not silent, that God is in control, and that history is not spiraling out of His stated plan. It's moving toward the glorious fulfillment of all that he declared to the world and promised to us.

The Glory of Christ Revealed

When we opened the pages of Revelation, the first thing we saw wasn't the rise of the Antichrist, the judgments, or the seals, it was the majesty of Jesus Himself. John writes,

> "I was in the Spirit on the Lord's day, and heard behind me a great voice, as of a trumpet, Saying, I am Alpha and Omega, the first and the last."

Revelation 1:10–11

What a powerful reminder that this book begins and ends

with Christ.

John turned to see that voice, and what he saw changed everything.

"And in the midst of the seven candlesticks one like unto the Son of man... His head and his hairs were white like wool, as white as snow; and his eyes were as a flame of fire."

Revelation 1:13–14

This was not the gentle Jesus walking the shores of Galilee. This was the glorified Christ: holy, sovereign, and ready to judge.

That moment should still stop us in our tracks. The Jesus who loves us is the same Jesus who holds the stars in His hand and walks among His churches. He isn't detached from what's happening in this world. He's actively involved, refining, correcting, and strengthening His people. Every message to the seven churches in Chapters 2 and 3 is proof of that.

To Ephesus, He says, return to your first love. To Smyrna, be faithful unto death. To Laodicea, repent before it's too late. Each word was tailored, precise, and piercing. Together, they paint a picture of the kind of church Jesus longs for: one that is awake, pure, and courageous in the face of compromise.

And guys, that's not just ancient history. Those letters are written to us. They remind us that Christ isn't coming back for a lukewarm church. He's returning for a bride who's watching and ready.

The throne room scenes in Chapters 4 and 5 took us even higher. We saw heaven's perspective, where God sits enthroned, worshiped by all who are in his presence.

"Thou art worthy, O Lord, to receive glory and honour and power: for thou hast created all things, and for thy pleasure they are and were created."

Revelation 4:11

That verse alone should wake us up. Everything exists for Him.

Then we saw the Lamb, standing as though slain, taking the scroll from the Father's hand. It's one of the most breathtaking moments in all of the Bible. No one else was found worthy, not a king, not a prophet, not an angel. Christ alone was worthy. The perfect life He lived on this earth made Him worthy because He was the only human who could fulfill the requirement necessary to pay the unpayable price. Only He could claim the title deed to the earth that humanity lost through rebellion.

When the seals were opened in Revelation Chapter 6, carried through the interlude in Chapter 7, and completed with the opening of the seventh seal in Chapter 8, we witnessed the sobering reality of the commencement of God's final judgments. This isn't something we can take lightly. The wrath of God is real, and the Lamb who was slain is also the Judge who will reign. Yet even in those judgments, we saw mercy. God gives warnings. He sends witnesses. He restrains evil for a time. He calls humanity to repentance before it's too late.

The trumpet judgments revealed that even in wrath, God remembers mercy. Every event John witnessed was another chance for the world to wake up. Sadly, most won't. But for those who do, those who recognize these aren't random disasters but divine calls to repentance, there is still hope.

Through it all, Revelation 1–10 reveals the central truth of history: Jesus Christ is LORD. He holds the scroll. He commands the angels. He determines the outcome. He's not wringing His hands, wondering what to do about the state of the world. He is fulfilling His plan with precision, love, and holiness.

And believer, that should give us confidence. It should also fill us with reverent awe. The same Jesus who saved you is the One who will one day open heaven and return in glory. There's no middle ground left. He is either your Savior now, or He will be your Judge then.

The Church's Call in These Last Days

Every generation of believers has faced trials, but we're living in a time that bears striking resemblance to what John described. Deception runs rampant. Evil is called good, and good is called evil. Yet none of this should surprise us. Jesus told us it would be this way. What matters now is how we respond.

We can't afford to live casual, distracted lives while the world around us plunges deeper into darkness. The Book of Revelation isn't meant to make us speculative; it's meant to make us faithful. When we see the stage being set for everything God revealed, globalism, moral confusion, spiritual apathy, it should stir something inside us to say, "LORD, let me be found faithful."

This is not the time to be silent. It's not the time to hide our faith or compromise our convictions. This is the time to stand. The Bible says, "Be ye steadfast, unmovable, always abounding in the work of the Lord" (1 Corinthians 15:58). That means we don't give up when it gets hard. We don't blend in just to be accepted. We shine brighter because the night is getting darker.

God has placed each of us exactly where we are for a reason. You may not have a platform like John or a pulpit like a preacher, but you have influence: your home, your workplace, your neighborhood. Use it. Share the gospel. Live with integrity. Show compassion. Pray for boldness.

If the letters to the seven churches teach us anything, it's that Jesus is walking among His people right now. He sees your faithfulness. He knows your struggles. He notices every act of obedience, even when the world doesn't. And He's saying to us the same thing He said then: Hold fast till I come.

We also have to guard against compromise. The church of Laodicea is greatly reflected in our current day, a church that thinks it's rich and needs nothing, yet is spiritually poor. Folks, this is not a time for lukewarm faith marked by apathy that leads to disobedience and a life that bears no evidence of true conviction. This is a time for the kind of devotion driven by the obedience Christ modeled for us. He first loved us, and that love should move our hearts toward compassion for the lost.

We are ambassadors of the kingdom of God. Our allegiance isn't to this world but to the One who will soon rule it. Revelation reminds us that every earthly power will crumble, but God's kingdom will endure forever. So fix your eyes there! Live for eternity, not for the applause of men.

When persecution rises, and it will, remember that Christ

has already overcome. Revelation shows us that suffering is never wasted. God uses it to purify His people and prove that His grace is enough. The overcomers in Revelation aren't super-saints; they're faithful believers who refuse to bow to the spirit of the age.

And that's what God is calling us to be: overcomers. People who stand when everyone else kneels to the idols of comfort, culture, or convenience. People who declare, "As for me and my house, we will serve the LORD."

So let's take this seriously. If Jesus commended small, persecuted churches like Smyrna for their faithfulness, He can strengthen us too. We are not powerless. The same Spirit who raised Christ from the dead lives in us. That means we can live holy, courageous, victorious lives no matter what happens next.

A Word to the Unbelieving Heart

If you've read this far and haven't made the decision to put your faith and trust in Jesus Christ for your eternity, please hear me clearly. You're not reading these words by accident. The God of heaven loves you so much that He arranged for you to be here in this specific moment because He wants you to understand what is waiting around the corner and how deeply He desires to save you from it.

The Book of Revelation isn't just a warning; it's an invitation. It's God reaching out to a world that's turned its back on Him, saying, "Come home before it's too late." The Bible says, "For God so loved the world, that he gave his only begotten Son, that whosoever believeth in him should not perish, but have everlasting life" (John 3:16). That's not a verse to be taken lightly. It's a declaration of love from the heart of God directly to you.

Throughout Revelation 1–10, we've seen both mercy and judgment. God's patience is incredible, but it's not endless. There's coming a moment when the trumpet will sound and those who belong to Christ will be caught up to meet Him in the air. The Bible calls this the blessed hope of the believer. But for those who reject Him, that moment will be the beginning of unimaginable sorrow.

Friend, don't make the mistake of thinking you'll have time to get right with God after the Rapture. Once it happens, deception will sweep the earth like a flood. The Bible warns of a powerful delusion that will come upon those who refused the truth. The world will fall under the sway of a false messiah who will promise peace but bring destruction. People will be forced to choose between worshiping the beast or facing death.

I know some people think they'll be strong enough to resist, that they'll find Christ later when it all comes true. But let me tell you, if you can't live for Him now when it's easy, what makes you think you'll die for Him then when it's nearly impossible? Today is the day of salvation.

"Boast not thyself of tomorrow; for thou knowest not what a day may bring forth."

Proverbs 27:1

The enemy of your soul wants to convince you that you have time, that you can live life your own way, chase your own plans, and come to God later. But later isn't guaranteed. Every heartbeat is a gift from the LORD. Every breath you take is evidence of His mercy. The only reason Jesus hasn't returned yet is because He's giving more people the chance to repent. We're talking about your eternity here. Make no mistake: God wants to add meaning to your life and make the purposes of your existence so much more powerful.

> "The Lord is not slack concerning his promise, as some men count slackness; but is longsuffering to us-ward, not willing that any should perish, but that all should come to repentance."
>
> **2 Peter 3:9**

Don't ignore that mercy. The door of grace is still open, but it won't stay open forever. Just like in the days of Noah, the ark was prepared for anyone willing to listen, but most people mocked and walked away, right up until the rain began to fall. Once God shut the door, it could not be opened again. The Rapture will be that moment for this world: the final call before judgment begins.

If your heart is pounding right now, that's not fear; that's conviction. It's the Holy Spirit drawing you to Jesus. And if you're wondering what to do, it's simple: call out to Him. Admit that you're a sinner who needs His forgiveness. Believe that Jesus died on the cross for your sins and rose again on the third day. Confess Him as LORD. The Bible says,

> "That if thou shalt confess with thy mouth the Lord Jesus, and shalt believe in thine heart that God hath raised him from the dead, thou shalt be saved."
>
> **Romans 10:9**

Salvation isn't about joining a religion or cleaning up your act first. It's about surrender, placing your faith in what Jesus has already done for you. When you do that, He forgives you completely. He gives you a new heart, a new purpose, and the assurance of eternal life.

You don't have to face what's coming. You don't have to live in fear of the mark of the beast or the judgments that will fall upon the earth. You can have peace right now, because Jesus is the Prince of Peace. He said, "Peace I leave with you, my peace I give unto you: not as the world giveth, give I unto you. Let not your heart be troubled, neither let it be afraid" (John 14:27).

I've seen people come to Christ from every background imaginable: atheists, skeptics, former Muslims, prodigals, people who thought they were too far gone. Every single one discovered the same truth: grace greater than their sin. You can discover it too.

So don't wait. Don't gamble your eternity on another sunrise. This moment, right now, may be your only opportunity to settle this with God. Fall to your knees, repent, and put your faith and trust in Jesus. Let Him transform your heart. You'll never regret that decision.

If you do that (and I sincerely hope you do), tell someone. Get around other believers who will help you grow. Open your Bible and start reading, beginning with the Gospel of John. Pray every day. You don't need fancy words; just talk to God like you'd talk to a friend. And when you stumble, get back up and remember that His mercy is new every morning.

If you've made that decision right now, welcome to the

family of God. Heaven rejoices when even one sinner repents. As you continue into the next part of this Revelation series, you'll see the full victory of the One who just saved you: Jesus Christ, the King of kings and LORD of lords.

The Hope of What's to Come

If the first ten chapters of Revelation have shown us anything, it's that God is fully in control. The judgments, the seals, the trumpets, they aren't random acts of chaos. They are the unfolding of a perfect plan written before the foundation of the world. But as sobering as those events are, they're only the beginning. What lies ahead in the next chapters will reveal both the darkest days of human history and the brightest hope for those who belong to Christ.

When we step into Revelation 11, the tempo changes. The world is trembling under the weight of God's justice, but heaven is preparing for the final victory. The stage is being set for the return of the King. The kingdoms of this world are about to become the kingdoms of our LORD and of His Christ, and He shall reign forever and ever (Revelation 11:15).

Just think about that. Every government, every empire, every corrupt system that has ever exalted itself against God will fall. The arrogance of man will be silenced. The idols of wealth, power, and self will crumble to dust, and in their place will stand the righteous reign of Jesus Christ, the same Savior who was mocked, beaten, and crucified, now returning as Judge and King.

That's where the story is headed. Revelation isn't the tale of a world falling apart; it's the story of a kingdom coming together under its rightful King. For believers, that should stir excitement, not fear. We aren't destined for wrath; we're destined for redemption.

> "For God hath not appointed us to wrath, but to obtain salvation by our Lord Jesus Christ."
>
> **1 Thessalonians 5:9**

The chapters ahead will reveal things beyond our imagination: a temple restored, witnesses proclaiming truth in the streets of Jerusalem, angels declaring the everlasting gospel, and the ultimate showdown between good and evil. We'll see the dragon's fury, the rise and fall of Babylon, and the triumphant return of Christ on a white horse. And through it all, one truth will echo: Jesus wins.

That victory isn't just cosmic; it's personal. Every tear that's ever fallen from your eyes will be wiped away. Every injustice you've endured will be made right. Every unanswered question will find its resolution in the presence of the Lamb. The Bible promises, "And God shall wipe away all tears from their eyes; and there shall be no more death, neither sorrow, nor crying, neither shall there be any more pain: for the former things are passed away" (Revelation 21:4).

Can you imagine that moment? No more hospitals, no more graves, no more wars, no more goodbyes. Just the radiant glory of God filling every corner of creation. That's the destiny of those who belong to Him.

And here's what I love: Revelation doesn't end in despair; it ends in invitation. After all the judgments, all the battles, all the victories, the final words of Scripture are still a plea from the heart of God: "And the Spirit and the bride say, Come...

And whosoever will, let him take the water of life freely" (Revelation 22:17).

That means the story of Revelation isn't finished until everyone who will come, does come. God's heart has always been to redeem, to restore, and to dwell with His people forever. That's what eternity is about, not clouds and harps, but perfect fellowship with the God who made us and loves us.

So as we look ahead to the next part of this journey, don't lose hope. Yes, the world will face dark days, but the light of Christ will shine brighter than ever. Evil won't have the final word. The Lamb who was slain is the Lion who will reign, and He's coming soon.

"Even so, come, Lord Jesus."

Revelation 22:20

Final Blessing

As we come to the close of this book, I want to speak directly to your heart, whether you've walked with the LORD for many years, you're brand new to the family of God, or even if you're still searching and wrestling with what you've read. The message of Revelation isn't merely a prophetic timeline. It's the heartbeat of God calling His people to stand, to endure, and to look up, because our redemption draws near.

To all my believing brothers and sisters already adopted into the family, let me encourage you. Everything you've read so far in Revelation should remind you that your labor in the LORD is not in vain. God sees your faithfulness. He sees the quiet sacrifices you've made, the prayers you've prayed when no one else was listening, the moments you chose righteousness when compromise would have been easier. He hasn't forgotten you. In fact, He's prepared a crown for those who love His appearing. The Bible says, "Henceforth there is laid up for me a crown of righteousness, which the Lord, the righteous judge, shall give me at that day" (2 Timothy 4:8). That promise is for every believer who lives with their eyes fixed on Christ.

Don't grow weary. These aren't the days to shrink back. These are the days to stand tall, shine brightly, love boldly, and declare the truth of God's Word without hesitation. The world may mock you, misunderstand you, or even oppose you, but remember this: you are a child of the King. You are sealed by the Spirit. You belong to the One who holds the keys of death and hell. Nothing this world throws at you can separate you from the love of Christ.

Let your heart be strengthened by the words Jesus spoke to the church in Philadelphia: "Behold, I have set before thee an open door, and no man can shut it" (Revelation 3:8). God is opening doors right now: doors to serve, witness, and influence those around you for the kingdom. Walk through them with courage. You have been placed in this generation on purpose, for such a time as this.

To the new believer who may have just surrendered to Christ as you read this conclusion: welcome. You are not alone. God has redeemed you, forgiven you, and adopted you into His family. Your past no longer defines you. Your failures no longer bind you. Jesus has made you new. You may not understand everything yet, and that's okay. You're beginning a journey that will transform your life from the inside out. Stay close to the LORD. Stay in His Word. Connect with other believers who will walk with you and encourage you. And as you continue reading into the next volume, you're going to see the full glory of the Savior who now holds your life in His hands.

If you're still undecided, if you're still wrestling with doubt or hesitation, know this: God is not afraid of your questions. He's not intimidated by your struggles. He's simply inviting you to trust Him. He is faithful. He is near to the brokenhearted. He is ready to save all who call upon Him. Don't ignore the stirring you feel inside. That is the Holy Spirit drawing you, reminding you that eternity is real and that your soul matters more than anything else in this world.

As we prepare for the next part of this journey through Revelation, let these final words settle deeply into your spirit: Jesus is coming soon. In fact, He may literally come at any moment! That truth should not frighten you; it should fill you with hope. The world is not spiraling into chaos. It's moving toward the reign of the One who will make all things new. The King is coming. The Judge is coming. The Savior is coming. For those who belong to Him, His coming is our blessed hope.

May the peace of God guard your heart. May the love of Christ compel you. May the power of the Holy Spirit strengthen you to live boldly, faithfully, and joyfully until He comes. And may you hold fast to the promise that "he which hath begun a good work in you will perform it until the day of Jesus Christ" (Philippians 1:6).

Beloved, stay watchful. Stay faithful. Stay ready. The story is far from over. In fact, the most glorious chapters are still to come.

A Note from Pastor James Kaddis

Before you close this book, I want to personally thank you for journeying with me through these powerful first ten chapters of Revelation. It has been an honor to walk through God's Word with you, to examine the majesty of Christ, and to see the unfolding of His plan together.

My prayer is that what you've read has strengthened your faith, deepened your understanding, and stirred a fresh sense of urgency to live fully for the LORD.

As a pastor, nothing brings me greater joy than watching God's people fall more in love with Jesus and stand boldly for truth in a world that desperately needs hope. If this has helped you do that, even in a small way, I'm grateful.

If you gave your life to Christ while reading these pages, welcome to the family. You are loved. You are forgiven. And you have an incredible journey ahead of you.

I want to invite you into the next part of this study. Revelation 11–22 is nothing short of extraordinary. It reveals the final battles, the ultimate defeat of evil, the breathtaking return of Christ, and the glorious new heavens and new earth.

I truly believe the best is yet to come, and I can't wait to explore it with you in the next book in this series.

Until then, stay in the Word, stay close to Jesus, and stay faithful. He is coming soon!

Keep Growing in God's Truth

Follow Pastor James for bold, uncompromising Bible teaching and up-to-the-minute prophetic commentary.

youtube.com/@pastorjameskaddis

instagram.com/jameskaddis

rumble.com/JamesKaddis

x.com/jameskaddis

podcasts.apple.com/us/podcast/calvary-chapel-signal-hill

Keep the Journey Going

Scan the QR code to watch Pastor James' **complete Revelation teaching series**.

Looking for more?

Visit **jameskaddis.com** to sign up for weekly devotionals & important updates.

www.ingramcontent.com/pod-product-compliance
Lightning Source LLC
Chambersburg PA
CBHW051615010526
44107CB00037B/1440/J